Dear Sam + Serena
With love + Blessings for
the future years, steadfast
faithful friendship
God loves you
Dad + Mum.

GROWING GREAT MARRIAGES

Also by Ian and Mary Grant:

Growing Great Boys
Growing Great Girls
Communicate

GROWING GREAT MARRIAGES

IAN AND MARY GRANT

A RANDOM HOUSE BOOK published by Random House New Zealand
18 Poland Road, Glenfield, Auckland, New Zealand

For more information about our titles go to www.randomhouse.co.nz

A catalogue record for this book is available from the National Library of New Zealand

Random House New Zealand is part of the Random House Group
New York London Sydney Auckland Delhi Johannesburg

First published 2009, reprinted 2009 (twice), reprinted 2010

ISBN 978 1 86979 145 2

Cover design: Bruce Pilbrow
Text design: Sharon Grace

Printed in Australia by Griffin Press

Contents

Introduction

This book is dedicated to the concept of hope; the idea that great partnerships are possible and that the clues to build them are within the reach of all of us.

'Life is difficult . . . a series of problems. Do we want to moan about them or solve them?' This is from the opening page of Scott Peck's popular book *The Road Less Travelled*. In today's world of failing marriages and short-term commitments it seems that many believe that *love* is also difficult.

So in the light of this we offer some ideas that we believe could be an antidote to that negative mindset. They are ideas we have gleaned and travel-tested over nearly fifteen years of Hot Tips seminars on Marriage and Relationships. We have seen them make a difference — sometimes almost immediately — to couples who are 'stuck', as well as add some colour and humour to others who just want to continue to grow and enjoy each other.

Just the other day I stood nervously before 1200 students in one of New Zealand's top schools, St Andrew's College in Christchurch. It had been a while since I had spoken to this age group in a school assembly and I wondered if I was getting too old to communicate to sophisticated and electronically savvy

> . . . the two great human fears, 'Can I love and will I be loved?'

students. However, I began by saying, 'Ladies and gentlemen. I want to talk to you about the two great human fears, "Can I love and will I be loved?"' The audience hushed immediately and for the next 30 minutes I talked to them about sex, love and hope. Afterwards the staff expressed their surprise at how well the young people handled my straight talking, especially how attentive, even subdued, they were as an audience. In fact that evening an extra 200 parents joined my pre-booked parenting seminar on the recommendation of these teenagers.

As I travelled home the next day and reflected on the students' response, I thought about how powerfully this deep need for love drives us human beings; how even supposedly mature adults will step over their children's needs, their friends' advice and their parents' perspective and cause havoc in the lives of those around them, if they believe they have at last succeeded in finding what they think is true love.

Many experts in counselling and marriage will tell you their sadness at how seldom they actually can stop divorce. They often confess that in spite of offering excellent advice as well as skills in caring and conflict resolution, if one partner feels that they have found a different quality of love somewhere else, there is no

> The most satisfying investment you ever make will be learning to love another person properly.

turning back it seems. Could it be that it really is 'all about love'?

Understanding the currency of love that is gilt-edged for your spouse, we believe, can be the route to aligning your life-dreams with each other and enjoying a marriage that is as playful, respectful and fun as it was during courtship.

It is the investment you make that gives a partnership value. People invest in stocks and shares hoping for a future payoff. The most satisfying investment you ever make will be learning to love another person properly. It will be the best gift you ever give yourself and your family and it will be the path to true maturity.

As a couple we are transparent about the fact that we have not had a perfect marriage. We have, like most strong-willed and passionate people, had ups and downs and hard patches. It is the big reason that we are so keen to hand on to others what we wish we had ourselves known from the beginning.

At our recent fortieth wedding anniversary, our children put on a beautiful dinner party with an intimate group of long-time friends. Our children made speeches that made us both laugh and cry and we looked back through the museum of memories of our life together with thankfulness that we hadn't given up on each other or on love.

Our eldest son, looking for a creative way to celebrate this milestone, went to a lot of trouble to choose a selection of special wines to accompany each course, and explained before pouring each why, in some way, it represented our marriage. As our son explained the reason he had chosen each wine, we were touched by his way of honouring us. We particularly remember the Mt Difficulty Single Vineyard Pipeclay Terrace Pinot Noir, from Central Otago, New Zealand. We understood why Mt Difficulty would describe our marriage! In introducing this one he suggested, 'The rationale was that great wine, especially pinot, needs adversity and that your journey together, as both partners and parents, in your chosen life's work, had not been all easy going or straightforward but that the adversity had brought real beauty and a quality that only challenge can bring.' He then went on to introduce Cloudy Bay Sauvignon Blanc from a vineyard which is a great example of innovation and creative ideas that have unlocked the power of an intrinsic New Zealand quality. He suggested that this wine was symbolic of the innovation that he thought we had brought to the youth work we had been involved in, as well as to our family. And finally we drank Veuve Clicquot Champagne from the Champagne House founded in 1772 and made famous by Madame Clicquot, who became known as the Grand Dame of Champagne for her values of modernity and audacity and her emphasis on quality. This for him he said, 'symbolised that faith, courage, passion and determination that you both brought to your life and to your faith in God.'

Although our knowledge of wine is scanty to say the least, and we will probably seldom drink such exclusive wines again, our son in his word pictures and descriptions of these famous wines gave us a resounding, 'Well done! — we children are both thankful and proud that you invested in your marriage.' A couple couldn't ask for anything more in life than an accolade like that!

And we believe that it is a journey we can all negotiate. It just sometimes needs new insights and the desire to succeed.

In this book, we share some of those insights. And we offer

them in the hope that those who have been where we have been; who are stuck, through lack of clues, may learn how to get unstuck and move on. We hope for others, who already enjoy a great relationship, that there will be ideas that add fun and new dimensions to your life together.

Without doubt the price of a life-long love is beyond value.

Ian and Mary Grant

CHAPTER 1

Marriage — the price of love

Marriage is the closest bond that is possible between two human beings . . . there is just no other means of getting closer to another human being, and never has been, than in marriage.

Such extraordinary closeness is bought at a cost, and the cost is nothing more or less than one's own self. No one has ever married without being shocked at the enormity of this price and the monstrous inconvenience of this thing called intimacy which suddenly invades their life.

Mike Mason, *The Mystery of Marriage*

When someone loves you, the way they say your name is different.

Billy (aged 4)

The deepest principle in human nature is the craving to be appreciated.

William James

'Most marriages are happy. It's trying to live together afterwards that causes the tension,' quipped a friend of ours. It was just a throwaway line at a party but actually his joke was closer to the truth than he thought. The challenge for two personalities to grow together into a lifelong loving partnership could be considered the Mount Everest of human endeavour. For those who achieve it there is contentment, satisfaction and many lifestyle rewards. As Ralph Waldo Emerson suggested, 'The glory of friendship is not the outstretched hand, nor the kindly smile, nor the joy of companionship; it is the spiritual inspiration that comes to one when he discovers that someone else believes in him and is willing to trust him with his friendship.' Marriage is the ultimate friendship. We were not created to be alone and so we look for someone who will believe in us and share the good times as well as the bad, all the time loving us no matter what.

But as individual couples embark on their quest for tender love and interdependence, there is inevitably struggle and growth. The process of exploring each other's personalities, motivations and joys can be an exciting journey yet this same journey can, for some, lead to disappointment and pain.

For some, who set out with great hopes, the challenges begin to appear insurmountable and these couples, instead of building the life together that they had hoped for, gradually build walls. Instead of their love growing it may metamorphose into anger, isolation and hurt as they silently retreat behind those walls, into individual castles.

We believe that much of this pain and isolation grows not necessarily from lack of skills in communication, but from the lack of *insights*. We all come into marriage wearing our own set of glasses and with our own needs and family baggage. The challenge of really learning to love is learning to understand how another human being ticks, how to meet needs and how to help the other become the person they were born to be. With the right insights, it is amazing how it is possible to break down walls, to avoid the potholes that cause couples to get stuck, and to have a real chance at growing towards true intimacy.

This book is dedicated to those insights. For us it took time and sometimes years to acquire the insights that have made remarkable differences quickly for us as a couple. But these ideas have helped us build bridges not walls and have changed some family patterns. Love has a price. It is the price that you are prepared to pay for the chance to hand on a heritage to the next generation. It is the price you are prepared to pay to hold on to what you have that is good, to gain self-knowledge and give up your own agendas. It is the price of the hard work of really learning how to love.

> Every day I put love on the line. There is nothing I am less good at than love. I am far better at competition than in love. I am far better at responding to my instincts and ambitions to get ahead and make my mark than I am at figuring out how to love another. I am schooled and trained in acquisitive skills, in getting my own way. And yet, I decide, every day, to set aside what I can do best and attempt what I do very clumsily — open myself to the frustrations and failures of loving, daring to believe that falling in love is better than succeeding in pride.
>
> **Eugene Peterson,** *A Long Obedience in the Same Direction*

The price of love is also about the investment you have already made in a relationship. It's about history. As Michelle Pfeiffer's character, Katie, put it in the film *The Story of Us,* 'There's a history here and histories don't happen overnight. In Mesopotamia or Ancient Troy there are cities built on top of other cities, but I don't want another city . . . You are a good friend and good friends are hard to find!'

In the early months of romantic love, Mary and I, like most couples, thought that we would grow old together; and that whatever problems we struck, would just work out. But it is more complicated than that because, in a relationship, whenever we get stuck for any reason, whether it is through a misunderstanding, an unmet need or just thoughtlessness and selfishness, we tend to close down on each other in some way.

We could however, think of relationship roadblocks as a gift; as an invitation and opportunity for growth and connection. Every gift has a price and our partner is often a barometer; a gift to show that there is something we can discover about ourselves that can be turned into growth and connection.

A young couple of our acquaintance, who had been childhood sweethearts, shared with us how much they loved each other and how well they cooperated in most things. However, they also confided that each Christmas of their six-year marriage had ended in disappointment and recriminations. Kate had built in her mind the possibility of generous and meaningful gifts from both her husband and his family. And Peter had got so stressed trying to guess what she would like, that he got it wrong every time. As for his family, they just missed by a country mile guessing what Kate would like as a gift. The couple finally decided that in future Kate would buy all the presents for herself. However, along with this compromise came the silent grief that she was settling for giving up on something that meant a lot to her. Their love was still strong, but the lack of insight into what was going on caused them to be

> Think of relationship roadblocks as a gift . . . see them as an opportunity for growth and connection.

disappointed, to get stuck on an issue and settle for sadness and a vague sort of grief for what they would never have.

After talking to this couple we realised that there were some simple dynamics at work in their situation. Eventually with the right insights, they were both able to understand what was going on and settle on a solution that was far more satisfactory than just settling for no expectations and therefore less chance of disappointment.

We have written this book not to be an academic thesis on marriage, but to give couples like the above some simple yet practical tips which we believe can make the difference, in a practical way, each day of their lives.

Most of us grow up damaged in some way. All of us are looking for another human being to be our soulmate, to fill the holes in our love tank, to heal the pain and make it better. But it will need more than our personal needs to find the path that leads to reliable, committed love. The challenges of finding and staying on that path are not insurmountable and the benefits are legion.

A lifelong partnership with one love has a multitude of spin-offs for ourselves, our children, our wider families and society. Married people enjoy better health and live longer than their unmarried counterparts. Children do better in every way when living with two biological parents. It could be argued that marriage is actually a child protection programme as well as a poverty protection programme, because children are far less at risk from poverty or abuse when living with two biological parents. Couples who stay together

> We marry the person we love . . . we must then learn to love the person we marry.

avoid splitting assets and income and therefore are able to provide in a more consistent way for their children. And finally society benefits because the stability provided by committed couples gives continuity and a resource which builds neighbourhoods, businesses and educational capital between generations.

But it seems lifelong commitment is considered less and less achievable these days by a society that values individualism and personal fulfilment above many age-tested values of the past. A newspaper report on the break-up of Tom Cruise and Nicole Kidman, who were in their day considered to be Hollywood's golden couple, began with the lines, 'Their love was meant to overcome the usual fate of Hollywood marriages. Yesterday their marriage was revealed to be made of the same tarnished alloy as the rest.' What a sad, slightly cynical and yet realistic commentary on so many relationships.

Well, this book is written by a couple who still believe in the whole falling in love thing, but we want to see happier endings. We want to make it easier for couples to stay together through the seasons of life and have several marriages during those seasons, but with the same partner.

So what is love? Does it start in the mind or heart and how do you make love stay?

Partnerships are usually kick-started by romantic attraction and passion. Those early days of courting, after a first meeting or a new fascination with a person you already know, tend to be surrounded by a cloud of warm feelings. The desire to be together as often as possible leads to outings, romantic dinners, shared adventures and the discovery of those things you have in common. And there's usually a sense of euphoria and hope.

I watched a band sing a song recently. It was about fearing nothing and letting love be your guide. It mentioned how satisfying this love was. How wonderful if another human being's love could really be so reliable. I wondered if the young girl singing those lyrics really had met someone who would faithfully supply that love year in and year out, in hard times and good times. I wondered how long his love really would be her guide and would be able to satisfy all her needs.

I often tell the story of a couple getting ready for bed and as the wife looked in the mirror she began to lament her ageing body from the wrinkles to the extra pounds she seemed to be carrying. As she identified the parts that she was so depressed about from her neck to her thighs, she asked her beloved to please say something positive to make her feel better. Trying to think of the right thing to say he quickly responded, 'Well your eyesight seems fine, darling!'

That story always causes amusement in an audience but it does remind us of how men and women often stumble around each other in relationships, second-guessing what the other really wants; sometimes getting it right and other times very badly wrong. Then having tried and got it wrong, they give up and settle for the self-talk that says — 'I can't win so I'll just do my best and hope it is enough.'

Yet how different that is from the idealisation that we carry in our hearts when we are looking for someone to love us. We dream of a partner who adores us just for who we are, who is sensitively responsive to our needs and will be there for us no matter what.

Certainly the deep questions in each of our hearts could be summed up as 'Am I loveable? And will I find another person's love to be reliable?'

Falling in love and choosing a partner, in our modern culture, is often a fairly random event. And it does not appear, in spite of our privileged lifestyles and environment, that in the Western world, utopia reigns in relationships. In fact the success rate for joy-filled lives within marriage is not high. Love and sex tend to have been separated to such an extent over the past 30 years, in both the media and society, that young people often experience sex but have no experience, or understanding, of love or true intimacy. Yet the dance of intimacy is probably the most worthwhile human experience. In rushing to educate the teenage population into a utilitarian view of safe sex we have unfortunately often neglected the relational side of life, which is the central core of our true happiness, leaving us ill-prepared for the reality of future partnerships.

Modern propaganda promoting permissive lifestyles collapses on one important hypothesis — that if the concept can't be proven to work out in long-term healthy relationships, it is not valid. Consequently we make no apology in the following chapters for holding on to the dream of long-term commitment in marriage. While acknowledging there will be 'seasons' within those long-term marriages when love and feelings burn brighter than at other times, we are convinced that the tools to negotiate those dry seasons are within every couple's reach.

As we say to young people, when we eat food, our first impression is the taste, but the real value of food is in how it nurtures your body long term. So it is with relationships. The sexual side of marriage is often like the enjoyable first taste, but intimacy and the ability to meet each other's needs is what really nourishes a relationship and builds loving partnerships.

Love – having more by being more

In their insightful book *Settle for More,* therapists Tom Merrill and Bobbie Sandoz-Merrill suggest that we as a culture have settled for far too little in the area of loving and being loved. They suggest that we 'expect' too little of ourselves; that after the initial best behaviour of the courtship and all the excitement and endorphins that go with it, we tend to settle back into our real self or 'who I really am'. This means we tend to reduce the quality of our behaviour and downgrade from the 'charming' self that we projected during that time of courtship. 'We gradually sink into our less public, more comfortable selves, almost like slipping into an old pair of slippers for the evening. Unfortunately, in the process of getting so comfortable, we allow our unguarded, previously hidden parts to surface and be seen.'

Yet if we looked at this syndrome logically we would ask ourselves the question — why would we allow that in ourselves? Why would we treat someone who has committed his or her life to us worse than we would treat the teller at the bank or a work colleague? And it is that question that is at the heart of the question of marital love. It is the difference between the *feelings* of romantic love and 'mature' love which is expressed and grows with thoughtful action.

hot tip ✔

Ask each other these questions regularly:

- Are you OK?
- What do you need from me most right now?
- What am I doing when you feel loved the most?

Romance and falling in love

Those early romantic feelings that come with falling in love are fascinating because they are not necessarily about the other person at all. The butterflies in your stomach and the sense of excitement and overwhelming possibility that come with that first love cloud are actually a *feeling* that you experience. No one really can explain it totally — it may be a psychological 'knowing' or resonance, and it is certainly something to be enjoyed and celebrated when it occurs. However, the reality is that we *marry the person we love* and after a time, sometimes within a couple of years, when that 'feeling' fades, we must then learn to *love the person we marry.* This is a different sort of love. It is mature love — the sort of deliberate love that needs another quality of character and energy. That is why commitment is so vital to long-term partnerships.

Commitment keeps us safe when we fall out of love

When that curtain of euphoria melts away and we suddenly begin to see faults and habits in our partner which had totally missed us before, we can panic. We may tell ourselves that we have married the wrong person; we can become depressed about our own judgement or let down by the feeling of being duped about this 'other side' of the person we fell in love with. However, if we are prepared to push through that feeling and acquire some more insights, then underneath that depression is another level of love and intimacy. You see, immature love says 'You be there to meet my needs my way', but mature love is different. It is outwardly focused and 'other-person' centred.

This is when we must begin to look at our love banks and at how we can begin to build real wealth into each other's emotional tanks that will sustain the love between us. This is when we can really learn what it is to be a soulmate to another and a platform for each other to grow.

The early exciting phase of romance will not be sufficient — unless augmented with an understanding of *gift* love, rather than just *need* love, and a common vision of what life together will look like — to sustain a vibrant love affair.

You see, many of us think that marriage is a bit like a box and if you get the right person in the box with you, then everything is going to be fine. And if there are problems, then trying with another person will do the trick. But we need to think of marriage more as a journey — from the early amazing romantic phase, through some rocky patches of self-discovery to the other side where we experience passionate friendship and true intimacy. We take that journey through really learning how to love, through learning how to meet each other's needs and through helping each other become the person they were born to be.

In the following chapters we would like to give some ideas and clues that will help you aim for 'more' in your relationship, retain the warm feelings and playfulness of your first love, and at the same time build a great partnership; a marriage that will be a shelter for each other, for your children and for those who are connected to your family through blood or friendship.

Why do we downgrade our behaviour?

Disappointment with marriage often comes in the guise of unrealised expectations, or even just a gradual move from romantic, sympathetic and supportive behaviour to neglect of each other amid the humdrum and pressures of daily life.

Unfortunately it's as if the more comfortable we feel in a relationship, the more we give ourselves permission to act our

hot tip ✔

Put in your diary your date with your spouse as you would any priority appointment. Then you can decline other engagements because you are already busy that evening.

worst. Yet to become harsh, uncommunicative or angry just because we have won the heart of our spouse makes no sense. It is unbelievable that we would still expect our partner to remain enchanted with us and want to be close, in a trusting relationship, when we have changed towards them.

The Merrills suggest that in recognising this syndrome we have the keys to taking a different, optimistic and hopeful approach to marriage. They suggest we can choose, in contrast, to see 'human nature', and therefore ourselves, as capable of so much *more*; of better choices, of loving and honourable behaviour arising from values based on the *best* that we are capable of, rather than the *worst*.

What is love? Understanding love banks

> When my grandmother got arthritis, she couldn't bend over and paint her toenails any more. So my grandfather does it for her all the time, even when his hands got arthritis too.
>
> **Rebecca** (aged 8)

Mature love builds things and has a common vision. When Judith Wallerstein wrote her research on long-term healthy marriages, in the book *The Good Marriage*, she drew conclusions from studying thousands of long-term loving relationships. One of her main conclusions was that marriages that lasted were those where the couple did not just talk about *sharing* a life together, but had

> We need to stand back and . . . look at what sort of life we want to build and with what materials.

grasped the vision of *building* a life together. These couples had decided on a culture of 'we' as they agreed together how they wanted to conduct their life together. They had talked about their life-goals, the values and principles they wanted to live by, how they wanted to spend holidays, how many children they would like and how money would be managed. They had also learned how to negotiate the hurdles or life-tasks that we need to put in place to build that strong partnership.

We each come into a marriage with ways of doing things; traditions and expectations, perhaps from our families of origin or from some years living a single life. If we hang on tenaciously to our own ideas we are going to drag along invisible suitcases into our marriages. Therefore we need to stand back and, almost as if our partnership were a separate entity, look at what sort of life we want to build and with what materials.

Love that lasts

You may have visited or at least heard about the famous statue of Eros in Piccadilly Circus. It is one of the symbols of London. The actual figure rises above a fountain made in bronze, but Eros itself is aluminium, which was a rare and novel material at the time it was sculpted. The sculptor was Alfred Gilbert and he used the fountain idea as an excuse for incorporating a variety of fish and crustaceous life in the design. The fountain was unveiled in 1893, and was warmly described by the *Magazine of Art* as 'a striking contrast to the dull ugliness of the generality of our street sculpture . . . a work which, while beautifying one of our hitherto desolate

If you only think about your love for your spouse, without expressing it, you may create love-hunger. Love needs to be expressed in a kiss, a hug or a touch.

open spaces, should do much towards the elevation of public taste in the direction of decorative sculpture'.

Now what really fascinates me is that heaps of people think this statue is Eros, the Greek god of romantic love. Yet the statue is actually dedicated to the philanthropist Lord Shaftesbury who devoted his life to the cause of freeing children, who were treated as slaves and often as no better than animals. Furthermore the figure 'Eros' is the angel of Christian charity, not the Greek 'god of love'.

So how could this love, the sort practised by Lord Shaftesbury — which obviously was a deep, passionate 'gutsy' love — be linked to romantic love?

In the English language the word 'love' has a huge range of meanings like, I love hokey pokey ice cream, I love my RAV4, I love Mary.

Ancient Greek in contrast teases out the concept of love through three different words:

Eros, which expresses passionate love, is related to sensual desire and longing. Plato refined his own definition of *eros* as initially a 'feeling', but with contemplation it becomes an appreciation of the beauty within that person, or even appreciation of beauty itself.

Philia was a concept developed by Aristotle and it includes loyalty to friends, family and community, and requires virtue, equality and familiarity. In ancient texts, *philia* denoted a general type of love, used for love between family and friends, a desire or enjoyment of an activity, as well as between lovers.

Then *Agape*, which is used in ancient texts to denote feelings for a good meal, one's children, or for a spouse, can be described as the feeling of being content or holding one in high regard.

Wouldn't it be great if we moderns could redefine love in its wider sense so that we treasure what we have, nurture it as a gift and build on it towards a lifelong partnership? We love the statement that one of our good friends uses about his wife of 25 years. He says, 'I'm so lucky to know Catherine, let alone be married to her!' There is a happiness that comes with humility on our part when we find a life-partner. CK Chesterton the genius writer and historian explains how there is a wonderful case to be made for 'humility' in marriage. A humble person goes through life thinking how blessed and happy they are to have this person in their life, how contentment for them is being able to share their joys and even to serve this person. Yet a proud person sees themself as deserving more and so loses the simple daily joy of gratefully appreciating what they have.

So can we suggest that the love about which we sing in love songs and search for in Hollywood movies may be only part of the story — as many celebrities tragically discover in real life.

The 'Aaah' factor

The 'Aaah' factor will remind you how to keep the magic in your relationship. Do you remember how you felt when you first met your wife or when she agreed to marry you or when you saw her coming down the aisle on your wedding day? I remember standing downtown waiting to meet Mary, when we were courting. I couldn't wait to see her and when she was late my thoughts immediately began to play out scenarios of doom. I wondered if she had had an accident and whether I should ring the hospital or the police. I couldn't imagine not fulfilling all the dreams we had. My thoughts went something like this: 'I want to marry this beautiful lady, I want us to do stuff together. I want to have babies with her!'

However, things changed after being married for a few years. By then I would find myself in a circumstance similar to this and instead of the joy of anticipation and concern, I'd be saying to myself something like 'Oh, she's late again!' What had happened to me was I had let the 'Aaah' factor fade.

The way we think colours our whole world. So look at your spouse as a special treasure. When I found myself thinking like that, I needed to refocus on the excitement of being in each other's lives and assume the best not the worst of her.

Setting some ideals

If we begin with high ideals rather than just our own needs and our 'who I really am' low view of ourselves, we have the opportunity to progress towards more loving and more satisfying lives.

But the key is to begin by being honest with each other and for that, many of us need some skills and some new insights.

We will look at how you can quickly discover the 'love' currency that will work between you. Then how to avoid putting the difficult bits into the 'too-hard basket'. These are the bits that we push into an invisible sack and then lump along between us, making do, yet giving up some of our dreams, all the time hoping that each other is doing their bit in dragging the sack.

The love that welds together the three types of love identified above could not be a better goal for a roadmap to intimacy and closeness. A love that continues to value the other dearly and to woo him or her as sensitively as when you were courting will be 'more' each year not less. It will demand less and give more; it will treat the other as 'tops'; and it will, most

hot tip ✔

Instead of flowers, send your wife a basket with goodies. Chocolates, a coupon for a facial, and tickets to a movie (a romantic one will get her attention!) and a coupon for breakfast in bed. Send your husband a coupon for his favourite recreational activity or tickets to an action movie.

of all, be honest and honourable.

Why investment is the key

Several years ago Mary and I were on our way home from a trip to Denver, Colorado, and while waiting at the airport Mary picked up a copy of *Psychology Today* magazine. This was at the time that Bill Clinton, then president of the United States, was the subject of very public scrutiny from the media for his sexual indiscretions. The headlines on the magazine read 'What Hillary Clinton needs

As human beings we are capable of more; of behaviour based on the best that human nature is capable of, rather than the worst.

to know!' Mary was fascinated by the conclusions in the article. The writer suggested that it is commonly assumed that when a partner in a relationship is unfaithful, he or she must not be getting their 'needs' met at home.

However, the writer refuted that idea completely, rather suggesting that a philanderer's problem was that they were not *investing* enough at home and in their marriage. You see, when you invest in something, you bond to it. When you spend time and energy on something, it becomes valuable to you. Just ask the guy who spends hours restoring a vintage car. It is precious because of the hours invested in getting it beautifully upholstered, machined and in tip-top running order. Ask the champion sportsman, or a competitive water skier who breaks a leg and cannot ski when he has invested hours in training and honing his skills. He will understand the value of his fit body and working limbs and feel his sense of loss highly.

Love just cannot be separated from investment and commitment.

What is the end goal?

Both men and women tend to want to make their lives count and these days we are all looking for more equality, intimacy and opportunity to pursue individual creativity and growth in our relationships. In the end by committing to making each other part of our 'life-plan' we can have those dreams.

It might mean a plan which looks at short-term flexibility of roles but which involves long-term equality — offering each other the platform to develop each other's gifts and fulfil goals, not necessarily at the same time but in sequence as children and careers allow.

After all, in the end, we all want someone to share our life's adventure with. Even the most hard-headed men and women want someone to share their joys and sorrows with. 'At the end of our lives,' author Pat Morley says, 'there will only be two rocking chairs sitting side by side. Doesn't it make sense to invest today in the person who will be sitting next to you then?' As well as in the children who are likely to be making decisions about our well-being!

Action lab 

- *Make a point of welcoming your spouse warmly as you arrive home. Say something like, 'Where is the most awesome woman in the world / the best guy ever?' as you come in the door. 'I have missed you today!'*
- *Do not go to your computer, or cellphone or workbench until you have first initiated this greeting and connected with a hug and a kiss.*
- *Look forward to each other's arrival and make it an event. Let your children see your delight in your reunion.*

CHAPTER 2

How to really love your spouse

> Originally, when you first fall in love, it is a thrill and surprise that here is someone who likes you.
>
> **Elizabeth Cody Newenhuyse**

> Love is the first requirement for mental health.
>
> **Sigmund Freud**

> I can live a whole month on one good compliment.
>
> **Mark Twain**

Enjoying a marriage – not just enduring it

When we meet our 'soulmate' we display such optimism about our future. Most of us feel that at last we have met someone who will understand us at the deepest level, and will meet all our needs. Perhaps this generation more than any other has created expectations of human love that are unrealistic. There certainly are those wonderful functional human beings who have grown up with warm affection and great modelling who have an excellent chance at healthy, giving partnerships. However, many of us are damaged in some way and are looking for a partnership that will meet deep needs. These are the relationships that fall apart when mature, giving, negotiating love is called for and when early feelings of ecstasy fade.

Those romantic feelings of falling in love, along with the sexual attraction and electricity of the first months, can create an island of euphoria. This is a wonderful time and we should enjoy recapturing it whenever possible. However, the tides of reality and time tend to erode that island, and it is often not long before we discover that those high expectations we had cannot be met completely by our partner. We discover that he or she is also a needy human being.

Romantic love, we are told, tends to last approximately two years. After that, reality sets in, as the scales fall off our eyes and we see this person in a completely different way. All of a sudden we start noticing that this person, who made us feel like we were walking on air, now has warts, eccentricities and even annoying faults. It is then that we may find ourselves experiencing an unexpected dread as our treasure island starts to feel more like a lonely desert island. What no one may tell you is that this is the common condition of many lovers during the first few months or years of marriage, as the heightened passion of their initial romance fades and they adjust to building a life together. (I heard a quip recently that marriage is the Jack Kevorkian[1] of romance.) However, there is also some good news that means when this happens we don't need to panic. As we intimated above, underneath that depression, if you will take on the challenge, is a deeper level of intimacy and passion; and the opportunity to learn how to really love. It is also the next opportunity for you to grow.

The differences

We don't believe that martyrdom (staying together for the sake of the children or through lack of alternatives) models positive messages to your children or brings you a worthwhile life. But we do believe in staying together, and we believe that with more insights love can be, for almost anyone, the way it was meant to be. It is the difference between getting off the broken-down train in the middle of the tunnel and getting to repair the train so that it goes through the tunnel. Real love is having a lifelong affair with your spouse!

It is often when that early obsessive love fades that we acknowledge that we will need some more understanding if we are to build a life together that is mutually rewarding.

hot tip ✔

- Tell your spouse what you love most about her/him.
- Be specific. Describe what first attracted you and then the other layers of character and personality that you have discovered and now treasure.

Research shows that a large percentage of divorced couples were actually very well suited when they married. So why does the dream turn sour? And even more sadly, why do many couples stay committed to the relationship, yet settle for something so much less than they could have?

The answer is simple and yet at the same time complex.

We tend to choose partners whose differences fascinate and draw us to them. But it is these very same differences that first attracted us to each other that can end up driving us apart. The fun-loving spontaneous girl may be highly attractive to a young accountant who is used to a lot of structure in his life and a plan for everything. But that same spontaneity may later drive him crazy as she overspends the budget and plans surprises when he was planning on a quiet evening at home. We may be attracted to the high energy and optimism of a partner and then be frustrated and exhausted by the magnetic field of activity and noise that they generate around them.

As a couple, Mary and I have vastly different personalities and styles. Mary certainly expected a quieter life than she ended up having, by being married to me. However, she readily admits that it is the optimism and enthusiasm that I bring to the relationship that is a foil to her potential for depression. We have had to learn how to build into our life her need for space and sensitivity. Her need for detail and quiet means she would become exhausted and depleted if she didn't have that.

Our differences need not be the dynamite that blows the relationship apart, but powerful energy that sparks creativity. They can be the flavour and colour. In any relationship each of us has something we can learn from our mate and each of us has something we can teach our partner.

I have learnt to enjoy picnics and romantic walks and to stop and explore different places when we are travelling. A real challenge for a guy who likes to get from A to B as fast as he can! I have learnt to try new things; and we have moved houses several times, because Mary is a natural explorer and creator. This has made my life rich, because without her I wouldn't have had so much fun. I probably would have stayed home and worked or built things and not played as much. And I have been the project man for Mary's ideas. We have been a great team and have achieved more and done more because of those differences.

Yet at times those differences have driven us spare. We have accused each other of them and verbally bashed each other with the extremes of them. However, we now value those very qualities in each other's personalities that have added so much to our partnership, and we laugh at the extremes of those traits.

We can learn to delight in compromise and negotiation. We can learn to really love. We can learn to understand and meet each other's needs and we can learn to help each other become the person that they were meant to be.

Every marriage is a different equation. Different but not wrong.

We don't believe that marriage has to be an endurance test or something that breaks us. We truly believe that it can be an opportunity for growth, celebration and love.

Marriage is about love and companionship. It is about making our lives complete. So, how do you go about ensuring that your marriage is a rich, rewarding relationship?

It probably begins by caring enough about your investment

hot tip ✓

- Commit to a day when you say nothing negative to your spouse. Think about what that would involve.
- Ring your spouse at work just to see how he/she is going.
- Ask if there is something you can do for him/her.

that, when you recognise problems, you then take positive action to rectify them. We hope that this book will give you some of the positive actions that you can take. It may mean being honest with yourself, being prepared to look at some wrong beliefs and choosing to take certain actions, rather than just living out of your feelings and emotions.

Only one partner wants to grow

Very often only one partner in a marriage has the will or the interest to do this. Our advice to you is to begin to learn and grow anyway. You will always influence the equation that is your marriage in some way, and you could be surprised how often in this situation, human nature being what it is, the disinterested partner likes what is happening, and is intrigued enough to engage!

Moreover if it is a wife who wants to address some relationship roadblocks, she can often engage her husband's attention by saying something like, 'Darling I have a problem I need your help to solve!' Men are natural problem solvers and if you want to gain his attention, then posing a problem that needs a solution is certainly a strike for first base.

In our experience, the major areas in which couples come to grief come in several packages that could be listed as follows:

- *The differences between males and females.*

- *Personality differences.*
- *Childhood and family baggage. These include misbeliefs as well as the way things were done in our families of origin.*
- *Lack of understanding of our partner's motivations.*
- *Lack of tools to resolve conflict.*
- *Lack of romance, recreation and fun.*

We are not psychologists and therefore have not set out to provide a complete manual on why people are the way they are. But we do want to give ideas that will help you deepen your understanding of each other and the enjoyment you can have in your relationship.

> My husband understands me. He accepts that, try as I might, some irritating things about me aren't going to change because they're near chemical components of my make-up. Home is where, when I go there, he takes me in every time!
>
> **Elizabeth Cody Newenhuyse**

As we described in the introduction, it really is all about love. People will do anything for what they perceive is real love and what they think will make their lives complete. The love we crave is more than just 'caring' for someone. We all know people who say they care for each other but still divorce. The love we all long for is the sort of love that makes us feel supported, alive, welcome and tops in someone else's world.

Consequently, having fallen in love, our greatest challenge is to learn how to stay in love.

Unfortunately a couple can have a bagful of conflict resolution skills and 'fairness' contracts between them but if their love bank accounts are not attended to, then a register deep inside them rejects the hope of happiness. If that register does not resonate that they are worthy, accepted and cherished, then hope for a future with each other tends to shrivel.

Psychologists who specialise in helping people regain love in their marriage suggest, that when they discovered this, their primary goal in counselling changed from *resolving conflicts* to *restoring love*. How to restore love is not just a rational issue. It is an emotional one and it involves the atmosphere between a couple.

Just imagine if every time you met a certain person you got bad feelings — you would never fall in love with them. If this person had hurt you, been dishonest or treated you with disdain in front of others you would avoid them no matter what. You would probably be repulsed by them.

Yet if when you met up with another person they always made you feel good, supported, and believed in you, you would seek out their company whenever possible because of the joy it brought you.

Therefore building genuine feelings of love for your spouse by doing those things listed above is going to be the key to staying

hot tip ✔

Cut down on your TV time

- Plan a TV-free night at home each week when you both do something quiet together such as read, write letters or chat about schedules.
- Set aside time for talking about goals, disappointments, hopes and grievances. Have regular KIT meetings (Keeping In Touch).
- Talk in an environment that you enjoy such as a favourite café, or just your favourite 'space' at home.

in love and revelling in each other's company. These feelings are built through deliberate actions, for instance breakfast in bed is a positive love account builder, whereas cancelling a dinner date because of a sports game will be a withdrawal.

The love bank account

The love bank is that mental/emotional recorder, deep within all of us. It works on the principle of deposits and withdrawals, depending on the kind of encounter you have with the other person. Your love bank contains many different accounts. Your family, friends and acquaintances make deposits or withdrawals in your love bank every time they interact with you.

Pleasant interactions result in deposits, and unpleasant ones in withdrawals. Attention, affection, acceptance, approval, fun and surprise all help to top up your bank accounts, whereas criticism, arguing and indifference empty it out.

Couples quickly learn that love is fragile and that it is the little things that count. And because of this fragility we need to make sure we make as many positive love deposits as we can; disciplining ourselves to reduce the love withdrawals, while building the habits of love as well as emotional wealth.

When your love bank is full you feel good about yourself and your relationships. You can easily ride through difficulties if your emotional bank account is brimful, but if it gets low nothing feels right. The smallest upset can be very bruising.

A husband who is taking his wife to the best restaurant in town to celebrate her birthday defeats the whole purpose, if when she asks if she looks good as they leave, he brushes her off with, 'Shh. I'm just clearing my emails.'

hot tip ✔

Reconnect on a date with some of the following ideas:

- Take a stroll in the moonlight.
- Sing love songs or read poetry to your mate.
- Give a back rub or massage.
- Dance together in the lounge to your song.
- Give a foot rub.
- Light candles and listen to your favourite music.
- Flirt with each other.

A simple idea that makes sense

In a recent interview on Newstalk ZB with Dr William Harley, the author of the book *Fall in Love, Stay in Love,* he explained to me the reason he *first* developed, and has subsequently taught for many years, the idea of the 'love bank'.

Dr Harley had practised as a marriage counsellor for several years when he looked back at his success rate and was surprised, as well as a tad depressed, to discover how low it really was. He then researched the general success rate for marriage counsellors and had to acknowledge, from the results of these studies, that they were not actually saving marriages — that instead of improving relationships, almost all of the couples divorced. He found that people who wanted to get divorced still did. Only one out of four marriages were saved through counselling.

So he set out to figure out what he and others were doing wrong.

What he discovered was that it was 'romantic love' that people wanted and would do almost anything to get. He explained that it is like an addiction. In fact the experience of romantic love is very similar to the effects of taking heroin and we all get it in that initial romantic stage; that feeling of amazing attraction to someone of the other sex.

If you are addicted to your spouse then there is no harm in it, in fact it is a positive thing. The challenge is sustaining that incredible feeling through the whole of a marriage. Divorces tend to happen when one or other of the couple looks for that love outside marriage.

As counsellors they had concentrated on things like commitment and sacrifice and conflict resolution. When Dr Harley experimented with concentrating on other things, he found that if he could help couples create the feeling of love then they didn't get divorced.

A simple idea that turned out to be profound

After many more years of counselling couples Dr Harley is still convinced that this is the key. If you do things to make the other happy; if you breach the 'romantic love' threshold — it triggers that part of our brain that releases endorphins and sustains that amazing feeling. Love units are the currency — basically they are the association of good feelings that another person deposits for you. Women tend to be especially capable of depositing love units for men and men can fulfil this need especially for women. It's as if the love of that special someone of the opposite sex is especially affirming for us deep in our hearts.

The highest-value love units rarely cost money. The idea that people with resources to do dramatic things like weekends away in hotels find it easier to deposit in each other's love banks is not

> The highest-value love units rarely cost money . . . in most cases women don't need diamonds but rather affection, openness and honesty.

the case at all. In fact, wealthy people often get distracted by the many things they are involved in. In most cases women don't need diamonds but rather affection, openness and honesty.

Men thrive when they are offered recreational companionship, sexual fulfilment and admiration from their wives.

Your spouse's currency is what deposits the most love units and will become obvious when you ask the right questions and are honest with each other.

'What can I do for you that makes you feel the best?' is a question that would educate you on how to make each other happy.

Now, Dr Harley suggests, his marriage therapy consists far more of helping people do what they may no longer want to do (begin to change the love deposit equation) so that they can have the marriage they want.

Everyone wants to matter

What makes people happiest is receiving attention from those people that matter to us. When we are married, undivided attention from our spouse inspires feelings of love.

Remember that everyone wants to matter. If you arrive home and your wife is chatting on the phone, and as you kiss her and put down your bag she makes no attempt to finish the conversation, you may naturally conclude that she is not excited about seeing you and that even trivial chatter takes priority. Consequently a withdrawal occurs from your love bank. Or if she is ordering something online and tells you to be quiet while she sorts it out as you come in the door, your feelings of warmth are likely to quickly fade — and a withdrawal occurs.

I often say to men in our seminars, it is not smart to arrive home and after parking the car in the garage go straight to your workbench and check out an unfinished project. Far better to open the door and call out something like, 'Where is the most amazing woman in the world?' Your wife's desire for connection will respond to the warmth of the greeting. She may say something like 'Not that line again!' But she will love you for it.

A friend who had been married for 20 years said she felt hurt every time she asked her husband why he loved her. His response invariably was something like, 'Oh I don't know, I just do.' She said that things changed dramatically between them when during a course he attended, he learnt that to affirm a person well, you need to be specific. So he began to articulate to her the various reasons why he loved her. Things such as, 'Darling I love the way you welcome people into our home. I love the way you make our home such a haven for us all and the way you talk to our children's friends.' She said she was amazed how those affirmations filled her love bank account. The feelings turned from hurt to enthusiasm to be more of those things that he loved about her. She wanted to be more hospitable to their friends and gained even more pleasure from creating a home that was a sanctuary for their family.

The wonderful by-product of this simple insight was that his affirmation of her elicited a responsiveness and warmth from her that prompted him to be more thoughtful, and soon there was the odd evening when she was receiving flowers that he had picked up — not just from the service station, but from the florist in his building!

No matter what facade each of us presents to the world at large,

Action lab

Keeping in touch. Get the time together that you need to fill each other's love account.

Daily minimum requirement

- *Set a time each day of relaxed debriefing to share each other's day and to see it through the eyes of someone who loves you deeply. It may be coffee in the lounge together after dinner, or a few minutes before bed. Keep this time sacred. Think of it as emptying the pockets of your day with each other.*
- *Tell each other three things that happened that day and how you felt about them. Even if it is just before you go to sleep.*

Weekly date

- *Set a date to look forward to each week. Take turns at choosing what form it will take. You may like to enjoy the idea in the box on page 47 of alphabetical dates.*
- *Have some dates that you do regularly as they are mutually enjoyable and others that you surprise each other with.*

Dates can be an evening out, a lunch together, a breakfast or a picnic after work.

If you have small children — then just a candlelit dinner after everyone is in bed can be a highlight.

Have some dates set aside to talk. Talk about those things that build your life together as a couple. Talk about them before they become issues; things such as money, children, dreams and fun.

we all — if we are totally honest with ourselves — feel an inner need to be appreciated for who we really are, especially by our mate.

Our self-esteem should not be rooted in our mate's hands alone. A person who is comfortable in their own skin is very attractive to be around. However, because we have chosen our spouse over every other human being, his or her approval and attention is very important to our well-being.

Withdrawals

You can do the opposite and create a hate threshold. You can experience both of those things in a marriage and can go from loving to hating because of the way you treat each other.

Professor Gottman of Washington University, during many years of studying couple relationships, concluded that what counts is not the number of fights or how 'in love' a couple says they are, but simply the ratio of praise to blame. Couples who say five positive things to each other for every negative should be OK. If the ratio drops to one to two they are in trouble.

The most dangerous female emotion turns out to be contempt. 'It's a real killer,' Gottman says. 'There is even a facial expression for it.' There is no question that harsh criticism destroys our ability to love. Gottman has found that men are much more affected by arguments than women are. When stressed, brains of either sex can flood; a state when messages go directly to the amygdala before going through the thinking and judging mechanisms. The amygdala hijacks control of your behaviour — you lash out and cannot think straight. Thousands of trials in the laboratory have shown that men are likely to start flooding at much lower levels of criticism and they stay in a flooded state, with all the associated negative

> Ridicule is toxic to a man . . . not being cared for is toxic to a woman.

emotions, for longer.

Therefore, set boundaries on what you will and will not say to each other, even in times of high emotions. One zinger can inflict real emotional pain and wipe out 20 warm interactions. It is not worth it. Tantrums really should be left to toddlers. Make a pact not to go there. The damage to each other's self-esteem and the hurt and pain will burn for a long time and will leave open wounds.

So when birthdays are forgotten or words of kindness are absent, she is left sad and depleted.

Mary would sometimes comment that I loved the TV more than her. I couldn't believe that she would say that because there was no way I would die for a TV set — but I would die for her. However, in practice, I was spending more time frumping by the television than connecting with her, and conversation and connection really mattered to her. Because of my busy schedule I needed some time to 'zone out' and de-stress, but because we had never really understood those things about each other and negotiated how it could happen for both of us, we both felt misunderstood.

In simple terms the love bank keeps track of how others treat us. When they treat us well their balance rises; when they treat us badly it falls. By keeping that register on the love bank in credit we instinctively know we matter.

Romantic love can be learned

> That best portion of a good man's life, his little,

> nameless, unremembered acts of kindness and love.
>
> **William Wordsworth**

As we are all aware, we need to keep our physical bodies fit, no matter what our age; and the same applies to romantic love. We practise doing this and, as with physical fitness, begin to feel better and discover new and enjoyable ways of spending time together.

Women especially need romance to feel loved. So recreate that first date or dream up a surprise date you know your spouse will love. Think about what you did when you were first enchanted with each other and use all your creativity to snatch moments together or orchestrate an opportunity to cross paths.

Researchers have found that couples who vary their usual date-night routine (visit new restaurants or try new activities that both of them enjoy) can increase their marriage satisfaction. The new experiences actually stimulate areas in the brain that are associated with romantic love — the same areas that were first stimulated when you were dating!

The yearly retreat

Take time for a weekend away that includes seclusion, stimulus and some fun. Plan this weekend, because without a plan it can fall apart on Friday night. She will be thinking, 'I have got him to myself for two days, we can share some meaningful conversations.' He thinks, 'I have her on my own for two days, we are going to have amazing sex.'

You may think that you can't afford this time away — but you must think about it in terms of the investment. If it is important to keep the most important relationship of your life alive then you must do it, because your marriage requires it. In the same way as

hot tip ✓

Alphabetical dates

Work through the alphabet on your date nights. Take turns at surprising each other with what you do. Some of your dates may be elaborate and well planned and others very simple, such as a DVD that you both wanted to see.

A friend of ours began this fun exercise by, on his 'A' date, taking his wife punting on the Avon (a river near his home). The next week his wife took him to a hotel for breakfast. Another couple walked over the harbour bridge for their 'B' date followed by coffee at BeesOnline. 'C' could be a candlelit dinner and conversation and a 'D' date just hanging out together at Dymocks for some quiet reading and coffee!

you may not particularly want to do your GST returns, yet your business requires it, so you do it.

Taking time away from your normal environment and your children is a healthy thing. Your children will benefit from your close and loving relationship more than anything you can say or do for them.

Modelling to your children the practice of love bank deposits for each other will give them the best training for their future partnerships. Showing them a good example by the way you behave will be an inheritance for your children.

One couple we know take their coffee into the lounge after the evening meal, leaving the children to be responsible for the clean-up in the kitchen. It is a great way of modelling to their children how important they are to each other.

Dad tells the children that it is his date with Mum and always says how lucky he is that she has agreed to come. Molly, their three-year-old, was cuddling up to her dad one day and said, 'Talk to me, Daddy.' He said, 'I am talking to you, darling.' But she responded, 'No Daddy, like a grown-up . . . like you talk to Mummy after tea!' His small daughter had absorbed the unstated fact that Dad is honouring Mummy by treating her as special.

So grab a lunch date together, or pick up takeaways and have a picnic tea.

If you are both busy people, build romantic pleasure into the chores. Do the supermarket shopping together. Treat it as a hot date. Build in a café meal beforehand or breakfast on a Saturday morning.

hot tip ✔

A 48-hour retreat

Take turns each year at booking the venue.

Make it a surprise and enjoy looking forward to it. Drop hints about the sort of clothes you will both have to pack, but nothing else.

Pack a getaway box with candles, some special lingerie, something to read and whatever else it might take to create a special time to be together and reconnect.

CHAPTER 3

Knowing and being known

It seems to me that Pol and I were very well suited being so different in every way.

Frank Muir, *A Kentish Lad*

It is the things in common that make relationships enjoyable, but it is the little differences that make them interesting.

Todd Rothman

The supreme happiness of life is the conviction of being loved; loved for ourselves or rather in spite of ourselves.

Victor Hugo

Professor Gottman of Washington University, who tracked hundreds of happy couples over many years (see Chapter 2), believes that he has unlocked the secrets to a successful

hot tip ✓

Think memorable – rather than just material. Remember that humour is like salt on food. It amplifies everything in a good way. It puts things in perspective and it bonds couples.
If you have to choose between, say, a new car or a family holiday, pack your bags. The car becomes routine over time, but memories of a good time with loved ones are the mortar in the wall of your marriage and will last forever.

relationship. He suggests that the overall key is that partners need to truly understand their other halves. 'Happy couples have a deep understanding of each other's psyches and are able to navigate roadblocks without creating emotional gridlock,' he says.

In our experience, many couples never actually get to the place where they really understand the other's psyche. They think of this partnership as a way to get their own needs for love and companionship met and they neglect to take the time to focus on the other person, to learn what it is that has made them who they are and what will help them most to feel loved.

Understanding each other better is the beginning of the journey of knowing and being known. A key to this understanding is knowing each other's life story. Everyone's life has been a story that has made them who they are today. A couple, when they marry, sometimes ignore the fact that each has a personal history and that each is a unique end-result of good and bad childhood experiences, sometimes of deeply held beliefs, anxieties and experiences that have shaped them.

Those couples who keep each other's *life story* in their heads are likely to be gentler, more understanding and more forgiving with each other. One young man told us that he knew that his wife had never had a man in her life who was kind to her. Because he was aware of that, he was mindful of his tone of voice and took care to show her kindness.

Another woman told us that she knew that her husband's first wife had used sex as a weapon. Because she was aware of that, she made choices that made him feel accepted and loved.

I am aware that Mary often feels unlistened to because of her childhood experiences, and she is aware of some deep insecurities that I developed from my years of stuttering. We take into account those irrational, but very real, reactions arising from incidents in our past and are able to show understanding of those needs when necessary.

These childhood experiences often create echoes from the past, which dominate our current reactions. However, by tracing the reasons for our overreactions, by taking them out of the closet and looking at them, mean they will lose their power to create the panic that they once had. A young wife overreacts when her husband pats her on the bottom, and works out that she

Action lab

- *Think of a way to show honour and respect to your spouse that is outside your normal routine. It may be making the bed with her or holding the door for her. It might be putting his clothes away or having a warm towel waiting for him after the shower.*
- *It may be the way you listen and speak together.*
- *Show your mate that he or she is highly esteemed in your eyes.*

was regularly spanked unreasonably and unfairly as a child. Her reactions weren't about her husband's gentle love pats, but about something else entirely. Another young wife panics if her husband is a few minutes late for a rendezvous. She finally works out that as a child she was left waiting at a railway station for two hours, when coming home from a holiday, because her father had been caught in an accident. Her husband now knows that her overreaction is related to that experience and he is more understanding and less ridiculing of her need for punctuality.

How do I really get to know what makes my partner, friend or spouse tick? How do I learn my partner's life story, so that I always have it in my head?

An intimate knowledge of your partner's background is invaluable when you are trying to interpret their moods and insecurities. It enables you to willingly make allowances when problems arise, to help your partner objectively see the situation as it is now, not as they interpreted it as a child, and to encourage him or her to recognise their potential as an individual. It may also help you to laugh together at past occurrences. Professor Gottman also suggests that couples who can laugh about situations and use humour to unlatch negative sequences will have a far better chance of a great future together.

We suggest that as early as possible in a relationship, a couple should share their *life stories*. This allows each of them to communicate, when emotional situations arise, something like, 'Darling, this isn't about you, it's about my echoes!' The common knowledge of each other's life story will give a filter through which they can try to understand and strategise ways to handle a similar episode in the future.

hot tip ✔

Learning each other's life story

Go for an hour-long walk. For the first half-hour let your wife talk about her life; her earliest thoughts and ideas about life. Her happiest memories, her worst memories; the people who were special to her and the people that were mean, cruel, or ridiculing of her. Those significant moments that had been life-defining for her. Her best and worst choices and even family secrets that she hasn't told anyone else.

For the second half of the walk (perhaps the half-hour home) your husband talks. Encourage him to talk about his earliest memories; his excitements and disappointments; those people in his life who affirmed him and those who put him down; his heroes and his mentors; his mates and his family.

The rules are that neither of you should comment on each other's life experience for several days. Take the time over those days to think about what it must have been like for them, growing up in the circumstances they did, and to think about their consequential inner needs or drives.

Plan a dinner date several days later to talk together about the experience, letting the other know that you have heard their heart.

Try to articulate what it sounded to you that their life was like, growing up.

Even if you have been married for many years, you will be amazed what you will learn about your spouse in this way. But how much better to do this early in your relationship.

hot tip ✔

As you turn the corner into your street each night, get into the habit of switching off thoughts of work, and switch on thoughts about home and your spouse. Think about all the things that you love most about him/her; about how she/he will be feeling; what they have been doing in the last few hours; and what you can say that will lift his or her spirit.

Seek her out. Engage in a 30-second kiss and ask her what the plan is for the tea hour.

The 'you're awesome' factor

We also believe that the 'I'm so lucky to be married to you' factor is highly significant in a happy marriage. Many couples are so busy fighting for their own needs that they fail to honour and praise their partner. They forget about that wonderful surprise factor that was so apparent when they first fell in love. That sense of discovery that someone you thought was just fabulous actually liked you and you could hardly believe would agree to go out with you and eventually marry you. You forget that amazing feeling of excitement when you picked her up from her flat for a date, or that sense of privilege as you saw her come down the aisle on your wedding day. You may even overlook the incredible privilege of waking up beside her each day; the privilege of sharing your life with another human being.

In Anne Tyler's novel *Breathing Lessons*, the heroine, Maggie Moran, recalls how she and her best friend Serena used to 'leave the dishes until morning' so they could be with their husbands. The dishes could wait, they thought; their men couldn't. As the years go on, however, the dishes start to come first — and the husbands wait, without noticing that things have changed. We need to work to keep alive the early feelings of romantic love that cause us to continue to seek each other out, otherwise like the older Maggie and Serena — we take care of the mess before we take time with our mates. Slowly we lose the priority of simply enjoying our spouses like we used to. It is sad to see older couples who don't smile or laugh together any more. Too many aren't saving the dishes for later!

Life-tasks

Judith Wallerstein, founder of the Centre for the Family in Transition in California, had studied divorce for many years and knew a good deal about its aftermath. She became discouraged from her many years of studying dysfunction, and decided to change her focus. She determined instead to study happy couples who were enjoying healthy, functioning marriages, hoping to discover what these couples had built into their relationships. In her book *The Good Marriage* she identifies nine challenges or 'life-tasks' that couples who want to build strong marriages must address.

At any developmental milestone in our lives there are certain life-tasks or challenges we each must experience (for example, the life-task of an adolescent is to create an identity and eventually achieve independence). She suggests couples with strong marriages have achieved the transition from independence to healthy interdependence by putting in place these basic building blocks for future strength and resilience.

The life-tasks that she identified are as follows:[2]

- *To separate emotionally from the family of one's childhood, so as to invest fully in the marriage and, at the same time, to redefine the lines of connection with both families of origin.*

- *To build togetherness by creating the intimacy that supports it, while carving out each partner's autonomy. (These issues are central throughout the marriage, but loom especially large at the outset, in midlife and at retirement.)*
- *To embrace the daunting roles of parenthood and to absorb the impact of his or her Majesty's (the baby's) dramatic entrance. At the same time the couple must work to protect their own privacy.*
- *To confront and master the inevitable crises of life, maintaining the strength of the bond in the face of adversity.*
- *To create a safe haven for the expression of differences, anger and conflict.*
- *To establish a rich and pleasurable sexual relationship and protect it from the incursions of the workplace and family obligations.*
- *To use laughter and humour to keep things in perspective, and to avoid boredom by sharing fun, interest and friends.*
- *To provide nurturance and comfort to each other, satisfying each partner's need for dependency and offering continuing encouragement and support.*
- *To keep alive the early romantic, idealised images of falling in love while facing the sober realities of the changes wrought by time.*

hot tip ✔

Learn to ask the sort of questions that will keep you connected. Try these!

- What do you need most from me?
- Do I behave towards you as though you were the most important person in my life?
- When I am with you in the presence of others, do I act in ways that communicate to others that our relationship is really important to me?
- Is there something that I am not doing that I could do to make you feel more loved?

More people are realising that good marriages don't just happen. It takes energy and a true appreciation of your partner for a relationship to survive and thrive. Maybe they are also realising that the price of love is immeasurable and that a lasting marriage has a high value.

CHAPTER 4

Building a life together

. . . It would be such a comfort and such pure delight to sit in sweet communion with you at such times . . . to talk of the future, of how we shall sustain each other in love, of how we shall work together to do good, to make a bright spot around us in the world.

Woodrow Wilson, writing to his fiancée, Ellen Axson, in 1884

We have no more right to consume happiness without producing it than to consume wealth without producing it.

George Bernard Shaw

Go confidently in the direction of your dreams.
Live the life you've imagined.

Henry David Thoreau

'Lovers are normally face to face, absorbed in each other; friends side by side, absorbed in some common interest.' CS Lewis makes that statement in his book *The Four Loves*. There is no doubt that many of the best marriages are those where the partners see themselves as friends as well as lovers, and side by side build together a life.

Building, doing and creating are energising activities. We can think of many couples who are driven by their shared passion — not just for each other, but for renovating their house or rearing their children, a shared hobby or activity; a love of tramping, sailing or skiing; or running a business, a church or an educational enterprise together. They love each other of course, but what really fires their marriage is the third thing that they both love — a third thing they're building. Many farming couples or couples in business share a life-work that keeps them standing shoulder to shoulder, purposeful, strong and looking beyond themselves. Work is the bone and sinew of a marriage. When we are working together in the garden, discussing how to decorate a room or running a youth camp for teenagers, it feels like real marriage — it feels like creating.

Anne Morrow Lindbergh and her husband Charles shared a love of flying. Theirs is a great love story but it is built around Charles's love of flying and Anne's willingness to be part of that. In turn she grew in confidence through his encouragement and love and after he died, she wrote,[3]

> To be deeply in love is of course a great liberating force and the most common experience that frees. Ideally, both members of a couple in love, free each other to new and different worlds. I was no exception to the general rule. The sheer fact of finding myself loved was unbelievable and changed my world, my feelings about life and myself. I was given confidence, strength, and almost a new character. The man I was to marry believed in me, and what I could do and consequently I found I could do more than I realised.

It is interesting that those couples that have healthy, growing marriages tend to talk about *building* a life together, rather than just sharing a life. In fact they not uncommonly talk about their marriage almost as an objective entity. Some have taken the time to write a mission statement for their marriage, or at least to sit down and say to each other, 'What is the "*we* culture" that we are going to establish?' They have moved away from '*what I want*' and '*what we always did in our family*', to '*what do we, as a couple, want?*'

The 'we culture': What do we stand for as a couple?

- *What are the values and principles that are going to underlie our life together? How are we going to work them out at a practical level?*
- *Do we have a great passion to achieve something as a couple?*
- *What common interests do we share?*
- *What different interests do we have and how will we support each other in these?*

hot tip ✓

Spend some time writing down the values and principles that you want to underlie the 'we culture' you plan to create.

Write a mission statement for your marriage. Let it involve your life's goals, your beliefs, your passions, your work, your spirituality and your attitude to friends and family.

Judith Wallerstein observed that it did not necessarily follow that people who had come from unhappy marriages in their families of origin had to repeat those patterns in their own marriages. In fact she talked about redemptive marriages, in which one partner experienced a different feeling in his or her marriage than they had ever experienced before. She talked about how, through choices and understanding, a damaged person was able to find wholeness and hope from a nurturing marriage as the couple worked side by side to build a life together.

It is vital that couples are reassured that our upbringing is not our destiny and that we can make new and better choices with each generation.

A young couple, both busy professionals, spoke to us about this idea. They explained that they had talked about their future as a couple and had decided that they were committed for life, and that that meant being mutually committed to the fulfilment of each other's dreams and abilities. They explained that they were committed to long-term equality, even though that would maybe mean short-term flexibility. In the short term, Steve explained that he may have to travel for his career, living in various countries for a few years, and Jenna is prepared to enjoy that with him while

hot tip ✔

Show your love to your husband by being proactive in making contact with his parents by a regular phone call or visit even if they are 'difficult'. A kind action or thoughtful communication is always appreciated and means that you are establishing a relationship as adults, not in a child role with your parents and parents-in-law.

they are young and before they have children. After they have a family, Jenna would like to stay home to care for the children and therefore she is prepared to put her career on hold for a few years. However, when the children are more independent, they are both committed to seeing her pursue her career, art or whatever 'she was born to do'!

Our life is a series of seasons and if we see it as that, we will be able to sequence our life-goals, as our energy and circumstances allow. We can gain pleasure from our partner's achievements, as a team effort together, if for a few years we are playing a more supportive role. In our experience it puts enormous pressure on a relationship if both partners are trying to pursue stressful careers while there are young children in the house. It seems that there always needs to be one member of the partnership who is free to take the cushioning effect when something goes wrong. There will always be incidental dramas in busy families. The missed plane, forgotten presentation or lost wallet. No one can plan for a sick child, an accident, a forgotten school project, or a child who needs support in some way. If we take the time for a few years to be the support system for our partner or family then it is important for the other to show real appreciation for the sacrifice and hard

> Our upbringing is not our destiny . . . We can make better choices in our own marriage

work of that caregiving role. Our self-esteem tends to come from our achievements and it is hard sometimes to feel any sense of achievement from those formidable piles of washing, from wiping dirty faces or from retrieving the bathplug from the toilet bowl for the third time in a day! Attention and appreciation are like vitamins for our self-esteem. Our mate's approval and affirmation is the reflection in which we see ourselves.

Their opinion causes us to achieve and see significance in what we are doing.

The '*we culture*' is the shared vision of the one life that the two of you want to create together because you are committed to each other. The '*we culture*' is the intimate intertwining of personalities that makes your relationship a unique, vibrant experience with a life of its own.

The sense of being a couple is what consolidates a relationship, particularly marriage. 'We-ness' gives your relationship its staying power in the face of life's inevitable frustrations and the temptation to run away or stray. It also gives you and your partner the sense that the two of you constitute a 'sovereign country' in which you make all the rules.

Some rules you might like to set for yourselves might look like these.

We will:

- *always speak well of each other*
- *practise courtesy by always ringing home if delayed*
- *try to resolve conflict in a way that leaves each other's dignity intact, including never going to bed angry*

- *never use sex as a bargaining chip*
- *never make important decisions affecting the other without consultation*
- *never criticise each other in public*
- *eat together whenever possible*
- *make a time each day to listen to each other*
- *make a weekly time when we date and take time for just us, to talk, laugh and connect.*

If you want a good marriage, commit yourself to achieving it at any cost – the rewards will be enormous.

> Affection is an affair of old clothes and ease, of the unguarded moment, of liberties which would be ill-bred if we took them with strangers. There are rules for good manners. The more intimate the occasion, the less the formalisation; but not therefore the less need of courtesy. On the contrary, affection at its best practises a courtesy, which is incomparably more subtle, sensitive and deep than the public kind. In public a ritual would do. At home you must have the reality which that ritual represented, or else the deafening triumphs of the greatest egoist present.
>
> **CS Lewis,** *The Four Loves*

Gravitate towards people who are positive about their relationships.

When you are in a relationship that commands loyalty and is worth defending, you will necessarily need to relinquish some autonomy. But as you learn to identify with each other and your marriage, you will more and more make judgements on what is best for your partner and for your relationship.

I was inspired by a refreshing interchange recently with a very busy businessman. We were trying to find a date when we could get together for a meeting. He was sitting beside his wife of 17 years, at the time. As we compared diaries he said, 'I am just so in love with this lady — and I have committed to support her and the kids over the next few years, because there are so many activities that they are all involved in. I have thought about how I can be there for her and I have decided to give her every Monday afternoon to herself while I drive the children around to their music and sports practices — so I'm afraid Mondays are definitely out!' How refreshing to hear this man articulate so well his decision to show his love for his wife in a practical way. You see, it has often been said that passion begins at the breakfast table. It is the kind word and the thoughtful act that builds feelings of love and responsiveness.

Never come or go without greeting each other.

Building a life together is also about traditions. It's about the after-dinner cup of coffee, when you chat together while the children do the dishes or begin their homework. Or the few minutes before bedtime when you 'empty out the pockets of your day'. It's about how you as a couple celebrate birthdays or anniversaries, holidays or Christmas. It's also about the other people with whom you share those celebrations. Your stable partnership is important not only to your children, but to your friends and your families as well.

Separation and reconnection

Traditionally marriage partnerships were never isolated from the whole community. Our grandparents would not have conceived of the extent of the individualism that this generation exhibits. Once we have established our new marriage as a unit, and publicly identified with it, then it is important to work out how we relate back to our families of origin. We are part of a generational cycle and relating in a healthy way to the previous generation is a challenge.

This is sometimes harder than it seems. Usually we have only ever known our family of origin and it takes a deliberate effort to readjust assumptions. Often a new husband will assume that his wife will just fit in and love doing everything the way he has always known it to be in his family. Or a woman will assume that her new husband will naturally want to join in all her family traditions, like Sunday lunch together. Yet there may be many reasons couples feel uncomfortable with each other's family traditions. These relationships have to be renegotiated and the patterns for your own marriage chosen. Your marriage is unique to your two personalities and it is an exciting chance to create something in this generation that will go on maybe for several more.

However, it is an act of love on your part to share those things that mean a lot to your spouse — like boisterous family gatherings, even if your natural inclination is to want to curl up with a book. Nurturing a continuous relationship with each other's families is something that you can both do as a gift to your children as well as to yourselves. A supportive wider family is what most individuals cite when describing what got them through the hard times in their lives.

Marriages these days do tend to come under many pressures from many different sources, and often our unacknowledged fear is

hot tip ✔

Set a date time to talk about your expectations for your life together. You can do this alone or with an older couple you respect.

Discuss some or all of the following:

- What good things from your parents' marriage do you want to replicate?
- What things from your parents' marriage do you not want to take into yours?
- Who will take responsibility for the chores? Who will put out the rubbish, do the garden, the lawns, the dishes, the shopping, make the bed, etc.?
- How will you bring up your children? How many?
- Do you want them to go to public schools or private schools and why?
- How will you resolve an issue that you can't agree on?
- How will you celebrate anniversaries, holidays, etc.?

that powerful outside forces, such as work, stress, pornography, etc. will overwhelm the human commitment that marriage demands.

Consequently clubs, churches and other friendships are all important in supporting your marriage, especially if things get tough. These other relationships are like a garden you plant. In the same way that a disease doesn't strike every variety of plant at the same time, the variety of these other relationships will mean that there are people in your life who will be encouraging and nurturing when you and your spouse need it. We are not designed to live as isolated entities but in communities of relationships and activities with others.

Setting goals throughout your marriage

When 730 marriage counsellors were surveyed by *Redbook* magazine about the most common problems that pull couples apart, second on the list of 10 was the loss of shared goals or interests.

Having goals and making specific plans to meet those goals is a great way to keep the fun and excitement as well as the shared interests alive in marriage. Together over the course of our marriage we have renovated houses, run youth camps, travelled, owned a boat, learned to sail, built a bach, exercised together in a variety of ways and made lots of friends together. All of which have made life exciting and interesting and filled with people.

Set a goal of learning a sport you can do together, or take some kind of class, such as photography, landscaping or cooking, or do something each year to enrich your marriage like a course or seminar.

Each of you make a list of goals for your marriage. Number them in order of priority. Compare your lists and select one or two goals that you can realistically reach in the near future. Be as specific as possible. If a goal is to have dinner together once a month, then get some dates down on your calendar.

Goal setting is a continuous thing, because we are constantly growing and changing. So don't be overly ambitious to start with. You may want to do a two-day tramp together or just have a goal to read a book together and discuss it.

As you can see from these challenges to building a life together, real life together is built on a lot more than just sharing a house.

King Solomon, the author of the biblical book of Ecclesiastes, is famous for his ancient wisdom. This is what he wrote on the subject: 'By wisdom a house is built and through understanding it is established. Through knowledge its rooms are filled with rare and beautiful treasures.'

Solomon is not talking about a physical building but a home of relationships: wisdom builds it, understanding establishes it and knowledge fills it with rare and beautiful treasures — treasures that make life full and meaningful. These are the things that even if your physical house is burnt to the ground or through some disaster is lost, cannot be destroyed:

- *Positive attitudes*
- *Good relationships*
- *Faithfulness*
- *Commitment*
- *Pleasant memories*
- *Mutual respect*
- *Depth of character.*

These are also the things which will build a love bank over the period of a lifetime shared together.

Action lab

- *Prepare a special dinner at home just for the two of you. Call it a cloth napkin dinner and set the table formally with candles and the best cutlery.*
- *Use this time for getting to know more about your spouse. Discover their future dreams and what they would like to achieve with the rest of their life.*
- *Make sure the atmosphere is positive and enjoyable.*

CHAPTER 5

What does commitment look like?

This is the age of sensation. We can act our way into a new way of feeling much quicker than we can feel our way into a new way of acting.

Eugene Peterson

Because of this a man leaves father and mother, and in marriage he becomes one flesh with a woman – no longer two individuals, but forming a new unity.

Jesus Christ, *The Message Bible*

You just get used to the disconnection. But we were afraid if we faced each other there wasn't anything there except being Josh and Erin's parents.

Katie (Michelle Pfeiffer), *The Story of Us*

Commitment is the rainbow of promise around a relationship. It is the promise that you have given up all other loves and you will do what it takes to make this one work.

Recently modern culture has moved away from the concept of committed love, to the idea that feelings should be trusted in all circumstances and decisions made on the basis of what is best for me now. In the Western world we have a generation of young people who are commitment-shy; many believing in keeping their options open. However, those who study satisfying love relationships tell us that the only way that real love can be experienced and the only way that deep love will grow is in the soil of commitment.

In fact this may be the first generation that actually separates love and commitment. Traditionally the falling in love thing was always linked to declarations of lifelong commitment, undying passion and eternal slavery to the other's charms!

This generation may have been burnt through seeing failures in the marriages of their parents, but hope still burns eternal and there seem to be just as many looking for real love.

The idea of commitment as a positive thing may make sense when explained in other terms. Many young people fear that if they commit, they might regret the decision because they have closed off their options for something better to come along. But think of it this way — whenever we commit to something for

hot tip ✓

On your wedding anniversary each year plan a special meal, and by candlelight, repeat your vows to each other.

If you have children, allow them to dress up in their favourite clothes as the wedding party. Your daughter may choose to wear her ballet outfit and your young son his wetsuit! That's OK! They can be the bridesmaids, the best man, etc. Your children will beam with pride as they hear you recommit to each other.

Perhaps you could preface your vows with 'I still do'!

whatever reason, there is always the possibility that there could be something better elsewhere. The reality is, that there is always an element of grief connected to commitment. If you choose one thing, you might never experience a range of other things. For example, you may be interested in both history and science but if you choose to study history in depth you will probably have to give up attending many interesting scientific lectures. If you decide to become a marathon runner you may never have the social life of a surfie. If you choose to buy a Toyota car, then you might grieve over certain accessories that a Ford or another make of car carries. However, you will never really enjoy this new car unless you are committed to it and enjoy the unique qualities that come with it. Actually, most men seem to be made for this type of commitment. Ask any man about his car and he will be passionate about it.

Anything worthwhile comes at a cost, and closes down some options for you. You will never experience deep intimacy in a relationship until you are prepared to fully commit to that relationship and let go all other options.

The key to real love is choosing someone with whom you can share interests and dreams and then committing together to the journey of self-discovery and building a life together.

Several years ago the American teenage magazine *Seventeen* reported a 10-year study of couples living together, conducted by sociologist Nancy Clatworthy. She discovered that there were more arguments and conflicts amongst those who were living together and not married. Her conclusion was that the underlying issue was insecurity. She suggested that for men, sex was physical and could be momentary, but for women it aroused deeper issues of security, home, children, etc. She concluded that it was cruel to arouse these desires in women without fulfilling them and that, *love without commitment is a cop-out.*

There is no such thing as experimental commitment

The public declaration of trust and fidelity expressed in a wedding ceremony is probably a major reason why marriages survive 10 times better than de facto relationships. Knowing that you are both irrevocably committed to making the relationship survive and thrive takes the fear out of minor rifts and spats.

Part of the security on which a marriage is built is that you are number one in the other's priority list. Faithfulness is mental as well as physical. If you tell your spouse that you will be faithful to her no matter what, then all sorts of insecurities fade.

It is generally agreed that for a woman to emotionally identify with a new marriage she must feel secure. That security will come when she knows that she is the object of his commitment. In the same way, moving away from obligations to parents and friends, and making decisions for the new relationship, rather than obligations to prior arrangements, is all-important to the survival and growth of the new one. When each partner chooses the needs and desires of their spouse over requests or expectations from parents, that helps the other to feel secure in this new relationship.

It's not that relationships with your mother and father and other family members should be automatically severed when you marry. But they do need to change. There does need to be an emotional separation, and a reassignment of primary loyalties to your partner. For some this is easy and natural, but for others it is very difficult to live outside the family circle and yet remain close. Family relationships may be, and should be, rich and deep but a marriage — indeed any relationship that is going to have a genuine life of its own — requires a redefinition of these links.

Jane shared with us at a recent seminar that she has had to come to live with the reality that her husband will always put his mother before her. She said, 'In the early days of our marriage, I fought it. I tried to point out to him how painful it was for me, that every time his mother clicked her fingers, he would respond. However, he couldn't see it. He was so brainwashed to believe that it was his filial duty to respond to her demands, that I have just stopped fighting it. But something has died inside me. I know that I will never be first in his affections and so, deep inside, I feel uncherished and unvalued.' How sad that this young man had not learned what the traditional marriage ceremony means when it talks about '*leaving and cleaving*'.

With each new generation we have the opportunity to leave home both physically and emotionally and to create a new partnership with its own combination of personalities and gifts. It will only be through a lifelong journey that the potential of that partnership is fulfilled.

Young people today are idealistic. They talk about quality relationships and want marriages that are better than those of their parents. They tend to want more intimacy, more equality and more opportunities to pursue individual creativity and growth. Commitment is the bedrock under the roadway to fulfilling those ideas.

Make your partner an integral part of your life-plan

Commitment to marriage is not a guarantee that you will always be happy. There will be good and bad times, joyful times and angry times. But if you are able to make a commitment to see each other as part of your 'life plan', you are more likely to build a strong, lasting, fulfilling marriage.

Commitment is about putting each other first, about treating each other as tops, about deferring to each other and keeping the 'Wow, I'm so lucky to be married to you' in the relationship!

In the words of Paul Newman, who had a faithful happy marriage for many years, 'When I have steak at home, why go out for hamburger?'

Say 'Yes' to your marriage . . . Love, at its roots, is a decision – not a feeling.

Periods of disconnection

There are times when you will feel there has been a short-circuit in the emotional current that holds you to your partner. This

> A man's great need is to feel adequate.
> A woman's great need is to feel cared for.

sense of disconnectedness will sometimes be precipitated by circumstances beyond your control. Commitment carries you through those periods of disconnection. It is the antidote to panic when for some reason there is pressure on your marriage from an unexpected event. There have been times in our marriage when because of a sick child, stress during an extra-heavy schedule, study or just physical exhaustion, we have gone through a period of disconnection. At those times, it is the fact that we are committed for the long haul to each other that keeps Mary and me from panicking. We both know that when the crisis or stress point is over, we will do whatever it takes to reconnect. It might be a weekend away, a quiet meal out together, or a drive and a picnic. But our commitment means that we trust each other, think the best of each other and are able to empathise with and support each other until that time is over.

In the first chapter we talked about investment. People invest in stocks and shares for the long term and don't panic when there are fluctuations on a short-term basis. However, disconnection should never be left to grow into separation.

Security in relationships

We all feel twinges of insecurity from time to time and the best antidote is mutual reassurance.

If you and your partner are constantly fighting about insignificant things it is probably because there is an element of insecurity in your relationship. Often, an argument provoked by one of the partners is not about the subject in hand but a manifestation of a basic insecurity.

What we need to hear from our partner is, 'I'm committed to you honey — no matter what. What do we need to do to get through this rough patch?'

This will offer a tremendous sense of security.

Husbands and wives may perceive risks differently: you may be able to handle financial insecurity while your partner may not; friendships with members of the opposite sex might be innocent to one partner — but a big threat to the other.

The best thing you can do for your children is to love their mother. The best thing you can do for your children is to love their father.

Security linked to our feeling of adequacy

A man's great need is to feel adequate. If his wife meets that need and makes him feel special and adequate, then her belief in him will give him security in the relationship. A man will always be loyal to those who believe in him.

A woman's great need is to feel cared for. A woman is motivated and empowered when she feels supported emotionally.

How do you make your wife feel supported emotionally?

Support comes through the little things and your attitudes; through acting with kindness and gentleness; through helping with the children, the chores, bringing home a gift, meaningful dialogue and warmth; keeping the 'Wow' and appreciation in your voice.

How do you make your husband feel adequate?

Your husband will feel respected and adequate when you admire his abilities, his body, thank him for his support and his hard work on behalf of the family. Tell him what a good lover he is. Appreciate his ability to address and solve problems, and enjoy recreational activities with him.

Security is the safety net under the tightrope of life

A major source of security is **commitment**.

Built into commitment is the concept of endurance — a concept increasingly foreign to a culture raised on instant gratification; yet a culture also hungry for connection and belonging.

In *The Luck of Ginger Coffey*, novelist Brian Moore describes Coffey's breakthrough into an understanding of committed married love. 'Love isn't an act. It's a whole life. It's staying with her now because she needs you. It's knowing you and she will still care about each other when sex and daydreams, fights and futures — when all that's on the shelf and done with. Love — well I'll tell you what love is. It's you at seventy-five and her at seventy-one, each of you listening for the other's step in the next room, each afraid that a sudden silence, a sudden cry, could mean a life-time's talk is over.'

hot tip ✔

Look into each other's eyes and both lovingly affirm that you will always be there for the other no matter what, and that neither of you will ever cheat. Ask 'What do you need to hear from me when you're going through a rough patch?'

Action lab

Set up a way to avoid the tricky areas becoming stressful. Use a system that you both understand and accept to handle your money. Start with some agreements:

- *Pay all your regular payments like mortgage, rates, electricity, etc. through automatic payments.*
- *Each have a discretionary fund which is yours to spend, out of which you can buy gifts for friends, shout a colleague a coffee or buy flowers!*
- *Have three 'virtual jars' into which goes the allowance for the rest (food; entertainment and eating out; haircuts, clothes, etc.)*
- *If you need to rob one of the jars one month in order to spend more on food, for instance because of a party, or rob another because you really want to go to an expensive concert, then you will know that you have to scrimp in the two other areas that month.*
- *When spending from these 'jars' establish an agreement between you that apart from basics like food, you won't spend more than, say, $100 without consulting the other.*

The reward of commitment

It is interesting that couples who commit to long-term marriages, even if they perceive themselves unhappy at some point in their relationship, have been shown to be considerably happier as time goes by than those who divorce. In 2002 a study conducted by the Institute for American Values in New York, entitled 'Does Divorce Make People Happy?', revealed that the modern idea that someone in a troubled marriage is faced with a choice between either staying in a miserable relationship or getting a divorce to be more happy was not the truth of people's experience.

Using data from the National Survey of Family and Households (a nationally representative survey with a wide-ranging data set looking at all kinds of family outcomes, including happiness) the research team studied 5232 married adults who were interviewed in the late 1980s. Of these individuals, 645 reported being unhappily married. Five years later these same adults, some of whom had divorced or separated and some of whom had stayed married, were interviewed again.

The results of these interviews were astounding. They revealed that a full two-thirds of the unhappily married spouses who stayed married were actually happier five years later. Among those who initially rated their marriages as 'very unhappy', but remained together, nearly 80 per cent considered themselves 'happily married' and 'much happier' five years later![4]

Action lab

Use a 'word picture' (an illustration that communicates with the other person by using a non-threatening approach) that will explain something you are feeling to your spouse. Use a story or picture which he/she will understand from their experience.

Emotional word pictures are a communication tool that uses a story or object to activate simultaneously the emotions and intellect of a person.

In this way your spouse will experience your words, not just hear them.

CHAPTER 6

Understanding the differences

Do you not know I am a woman? When I think, I must speak.

William Shakespeare, *As You Like It*

The first duty of love is to listen.

Paul Tillich, theologian

One of the best hearing aids a man can have is a woman.

Groucho Marx, movie actor

In reality, every marriage is two marriages — the wife's marriage and the husband's marriage. Or, as someone once said, marriage is a two-storey house — her story and his story.

Communication and miscommunication – husbands and wives

> To listen to another's soul into a condition of disclosure and discovery may be almost the greatest service that any human being performs for another.
>
> **Reuel Howe,** *The Miracle of Dialogue*

A general summary of differences between men and women would be recognisable by most couples. Here are just a few.

Travelling

When men go on a journey their goal tends to be to get from A to B as quickly as possible, whereas women tend to want to take in and enjoy the experiences along the way. Often I talk to teenagers in high school assemblies about these differences. I say, 'You know what it is like when you are going on a trip. Dad says something like "Tomorrow we are off on our holiday to Christchurch and we need to be in Wellington in time to catch the inter-island ferry. The trip will take 12 hours so we need to be in the car at six o'clock tomorrow morning . . . Remember I don't mean five past six — I mean six o'clock! Does everyone understand me? Now at five to six next morning, what is Mum doing? She is rushing around the house checking that everything is tidy and nothing has been forgotten. Whereas Dad is in the car honking the horn saying, "We've got four minutes to go!"

'An hour down the road little Johnny in the backseat says, "I want to go to the toilet." Dad looks at Mum and says, "Why don't you train the kids to go to the toilet before they get into the car?"

'Think of it . . . he's not even owning his own flesh and blood! Because his head is focused solely on where he is going, he is not wanting to be distracted by toilet stops. Sometime later he still hasn't stopped and Mum persists they can't wait any longer. Dad says, "If we stop now, all the caravans and trucks will pass us and then we will get them on the hills!"'

There is usually a burst of laughter from the teenagers in the room as they recognise their dad in the scenario.

Later I suggest when they stop for a meal break, that it is wise not to sit Dad in the window of the café. Otherwise he will see all the other cars going by and hurry the family, 'Quick eat up, eat up, we have got to keep moving.' You see, he is on a mission. Usually Mum just wants to enjoy the journey.

We were in Sydney for a few days conducting a seminar, when Mary picked up an advertisement in the *Sydney Morning Herald* for a tourist group for widows. The byline was, 'We'll let you stop at all the places your late husband wouldn't let you stop at.'

I love the story of the couple travelling through Europe. He says to her, 'Come on, if we keep stopping we'll never get to see Europe!' Now think that one through.

Shopping

Then there is the way that men and women go shopping. Men tend to go shopping but women go sho..o . . . o..ppp..p..ping. I am sure all blokes have done what I have done. You decide to be

Action lab

- *Practise asking questions of your spouse that will build intimacy.*
- *Think about a question that will inspire not only a response, but will open your spouse's soul.*

the loving, responsive husband and you go with your wife when she is wanting to buy a new top. She goes into the dressing room and appears shortly in a blouse, looking for your approval and feedback. I used to say, 'Not bad.' I have since learned that they are completely the wrong words. The words should be 'Awesome, babe'. Otherwise she will go back and try another top, and another one, and by the time she has reached the eighth one, you become like a crazed animal. You can 'see' yourself crashing through the plate-glass window to escape. And why? Because men are basically 'hunters'. They are geared to 'Shoot it, bag it, then take it home'! Women are usually far better shoppers than men because they take time and care researching their acquisitions. Just ask any shoe-shop assistant how many pairs of shoes their female customers try, on average, before they make a purchase.

Sex

Next we come to the whole area of 'lovemaking'. Men are like microwaves; women are more like crockpots. 'Wham bam thank you ma'am' is an old saying that came from the fact that men, if they wanted to, could be ready for sex quickly and then move on quickly. 'Thank you very much for a lovely time' was the sentiment behind the saying! However, both men and women enjoy far greater intimacy when they understand and allow for each other's needs. For women sex is associated with much deeper emotions. They tend to need closeness involving words, atmosphere and affection before they want to have sex. Think about it — a young husband can have an argument with his wife and then say 'Sorry', followed by 'Let's make love'. Yet unless he has shown real remorse and kindness, taking time to make up for his harsh words and criticism, she will not be wanting to be intimate with him. We

Men tend to want to have sex to feel close to their wives whereas their wives don't want to have sex until they *feel* close.

use the word 'young' because husbands tend to learn this dynamic very quickly even though they may not understand it!

At the same time, if a wife brushes off her husband's attempts to express love through his sexual advances, he is likely to feel rejected and isolated.

Men tend to want to have sex to feel close to their wives whereas their wives don't want to have sex until they *feel* close.

In some ways it is amazing that men and women ever get together because their styles are so different. So that is the challenge: a marriage must be a journey towards understanding each other's needs and meeting them.

Communication and mutual responsiveness

One of the biggest challenges for marriage is to establish the sort of communication that is mutually understanding of the other's style and needs. Many women need words, atmosphere and romance before they are likely to respond physically to their spouse. Women can be very sensitive to their tone of voice. A husband's softness and kindness can turn his wife on emotionally and sexually and his gruffness or meanness can turn her off. For a woman, communication is the key to responsiveness in all other areas of a relationship.

A man can be working in his workshop and think about making love to his wife and expect her to feel the same. But for a woman, the kind words he said at breakfast time, the thoughtful phone call

> The tone of a man's voice is sexual to his wife . . . his words affect her emotional and sexual responsiveness.

he made at lunch time to share some news and say he was thinking about her, and the fantastic greeting he gave her as he arrived home are all so important. If your communication is underpinned by that 'Wow, I'm so lucky' attitude, then you will always try to listen with love and always try to speak with love.

The word count mismatch

The fact is men and women think, feel and behave differently and they do so from birth. Even at kindergarten little boys are noisier, whereas little girls tend to play more cooperatively. A University of Edinburgh behavioural study revealed that noises produced by baby girls were 100 per cent conversational. Baby boys scored a mere 51 per cent. The other sounds that the little boys made were just noises, most of them motor noises! Not surprisingly, when these little girls grow up, they are more verbal.

As adults men generally use far fewer words a day than women do. Women, it is suggested, use 20–25,000 words a day (although most men would swear it was zillions more), whereas men use a mere 12–14,000 words a day. That can be a problem when, at the end of the day, a wife wants to unwind by talking about her day and her mate wants to unwind by not talking!

It is helpful to know what is needed

It has been said that women decide what they think by talking

You may like to consider yourself as honoured to be chosen out of all the men in the world to be her sounding board!

about it, whereas men usually don't want to talk until they know what they think.

Husbands, you can actually think of this as very flattering when your wife wants to decide what she thinks about something by talking to you. You may like to consider yourself honoured to be chosen out of all the men in the world to be her sounding board!

Remember, for your wife the feeling of being listened to is so close to the feeling of being loved that she often can't tell the difference. So turn off the TV and talk! That will be a gift of love that you give to her.

Men, even though you haven't got as many words in your 'wordbag', try to save a few thousand words for home!

Give them to your wife as a gift, and if you really are too exhausted to talk, then just ask questions and listen.

Men's and women's brains

In their book *Men are Like Waffles — Women are Like Spaghetti*, Bill and Pam Farrel explain how men and women process things differently. In the way that a plate of spaghetti is made up of lots of different strands, touching and intertwining with each other, women process life through these interconnections. If you follow a noodle around the plate you will see that it intercepts with a lot of others and may even join seamlessly with another. They say that women process life in this way; every thought and issue is connected to every other thought and issue in some way. They suggest, 'Life is more of a process for women than it is for men. This is why women are typically better at multitasking . . . She can talk on the phone, prepare a meal, write a shopping list, work on the agenda for tomorrow's business meeting, talk to her children as they are going out to play and close the door with her foot without skipping a beat . . . Because all her thoughts, emotions and beliefs are connected she is able to process more information and keep track of more activities.' Women problem solve in a very different way from men.

Men's brains tend to be geared to work in a more compartmentalised way. Thus the word picture they use is the squares of a waffle. If Dad is cooking the barbecue we suggest that you don't engage him in meaningful conversation, because he is focused on the one thing — getting the meat cooked. Men can generally focus on tasks very well and do not notice distractions. The Farrels explain how men will go into one square and work on that one issue at a time, before coming out of the square and going into another. They say, 'There are even some squares that men go into where they are thinking about nothing at all. It is hard for women to imagine that — but they do. That is why men sometimes feel in overload when women are telling them a story about their day that is connected to a whole lot of relationships and situations. He is jumping between squares trying to keep up!'

> A man is not idle because he is absorbed in thought. There is a visible labour and there is an invisible labour.
>
> **Victor Hugo**

Men can channel their problem-solving skills

A man will usually feel the need to try to solve his wife's problems, but if he can just listen without trying to fix things, she will feel deeply understood. Stephen, a young friend who is a business consultant, told us recently how each evening his young wife would pour out her frustrations and problems with her job. He, out of love for her, would put on his consulting 'hat' and work out a strategy for her to follow. He was bewildered by her response. She said something equivalent to 'Don't lecture me. I don't want advice. I just want you to listen. I don't need rescuing; I just want a sounding board.' He said, 'I am learning to use phrases like "Tell me about it", followed by "What do you think are your options?" Or, "Anything else?" She now knows that I will contribute my solutions if she asks for them, otherwise I let her work out her own solutions as she talks!'

However, a man will want to be acknowledged for what he considers to be his contribution. If a wife is appreciative of that, then he will feel affirmed and is likely to take real responsibility. Males are Mr Fix-its and when faced with a problem to solve most will readily volunteer to undertake a task or alter behaviour.

Men and feelings

Men have a harder time sharing their feelings than women do. Men tend to share what they think rather than what they feel. While this is not always a negative (his strength and objectivity can be truly helpful to his wife), he will need safe places to unburden his feelings without exposing himself to ridicule. Boys tend to grow up learning the lesson well that to avoid ridicule by their male peers they need to be stoic and not appear weak or, in colloquial Kiwi blokes' language, a 'girl's blouse'! This fear of ridicule and his desire to solve his own problems before he talks about them will often cause misunderstandings. Create safety for your mate by reassuring him that you will not talk to others about his personal revelations about how he is feeling without his permission.

Female friendships for women and male friendships for men

A woman is likely to feel frustrated if she relies on her husband for all her conversational needs. Men just generally don't have the word power, or even sometimes the listening power. Women need to enjoy their female friendships and conversations and 'chew the cud', as it were, over coffee with girlfriends as they are working out what they think.

Seek out the company of other women in clubs and social groups. That side of your life is important and should be enjoyed.

In the same way, men need to do men's things with other men. They need to play competitive sports and enjoy the less communicative comradeship of other men's company. Experts tell us that if men don't enjoy some male friendships that involve companionable activities, and instead rely solely on their wife for their emotional needs, then they will have some level of sexual dysfunction. It is a positive thing to enjoy healthy friendships of the same sex.

A relationship must breathe to survive

A relationship that doesn't allow for healthy friendships outside the marriage and doesn't allow the individuals within it to grow will go sour over time because of the lack of air.

A successful relationship is one that creates a true sense of togetherness but also allows each partner their own space, to avoid

hot tip ✓

- Keep the fun and romance in your dates.
- Employ a regular babysitter. Think of what you would do to impress, if this were the first time you had ever taken each other out. Send a surprise card with movie tickets enclosed.
- Make some dates surprises, and others just your favourite café or an outing to watch the sunset from your favourite spot.
- Enjoy even a simple pleasure such as spending the evening together at the local bookshop. Drink coffee or hot chocolate and then browse around the store enjoying the atmosphere and each other's company.
- Have a positive attitude. 'Our relationship really matters. We're going to have a great time!'

emotional claustrophobia.

We all want to enjoy true intimacy with our partner. And we all want our own space. The problem lies in establishing a healthy balance between too much closeness, which can be suffocating, and too much distance, leaving one partner feeling shut out. Your relationship will be supported by the other activities that both of you engage in: the hobbies, the sport, the social life, your church, your friends and family all contribute to your well-being and sense of connectedness.

When your marriage is under stress, it is often these other dimensions in your life that will support you through. In the same way, the love and support of a committed partner can be the very platform of encouragement we need to take a step towards pursuing those interests and abilities that we long to develop.

We all need to ask ourselves 'What makes my heart sing? What was I born to do?' As we pursue our own creativity and dreams we will bring interests and friends into our marriages.

It is vital to the health of your relationship that both you and your partner fulfil your ambitions. A mother may put aside her own career goals for a few years while child rearing, but it is important for her to rediscover her own potential and ability. In the meantime, it is important for her to explore other areas of interest that are open to her during these years. We are more interesting people when we are growing and learning and becoming all that we were meant to be.

Pace yourself. Our lives tend to go in waves or seasons. Your energy will return as your children become less physically demanding. Give yourself time out. Don't try to do everything at once and burn yourself out. Work within your own energy levels.

Some emotional needs will be met within your marriage; others, outside your relationship. You need to realise and accept that your partner can't take care of all your needs. Depending on your partner alone for your happiness is unhealthy because you are committing yourself to emotional slavery. You must learn to have confidence in yourself and recognise that interdependence is far healthier than total dependence.

In the situation when a wife is currently not working outside the home, she may feel lonely and lack emotional support. Her husband may feel a lot of pressure, both internal and external through his job. His self-esteem hangs on the way he handles his business, and the status of the entire family depends on his success. By the time he gets home at night, he often has little left with which to prop up his lonely wife . . . even if he understands her.

If you try to depend on this man to satisfy all your needs, you will be continually frustrated by his failure to deliver.

Instead you must achieve a network of women friends with whom you can talk, laugh, gripe, dream and recreate. There are many wives and mothers around you who have the same needs and experiences. They will be looking for you in the same way you are searching for them.

We all have different needs — some of us need fun, some of us need lots of talking, some of us need the stimulation of art and some of us need solitude. Your partner *should* meet many of the needs in your life — but he or she can't meet *all* of them.

What is healthy communication between husbands and wives?

So what sort of communication should men and women enjoy within a marriage? Well, they should enjoy quality communication. A set time each day to talk and share. The average home needs an hour of quality conversation each day. Like watering a garden, meaningful connection takes time. Many spouses drift apart because they don't know each other any more. They don't know about each other's thoughts, dreams, faith and day-to-day lives.

Our sons will get their view of women by the way we talk to their mother. Our daughters will craft their view of men by the way we talk to their father.

Connect with each other as you arrive home with a de-stressing hug and take a minute to reconnect with each other's world.

Miscommunication between men and women on how they de-stress

In our modern world many couples have dual careers that create unique stresses. By the end of the day both can be exhausted and depleted but have different needs for addressing that exhaustion.

A man will usually de-stress by retreating and going into a mental 'cave' which may take the form of reading the paper, watching TV, going to the computer, etc. However, a woman is more likely to need some sort of physical touch and hug in order to de-stress. According to Dr John Gray of *Men are from Mars* fame, the testosterone that women need to push through in a competitive corporate or working environment depletes her, whereas that same testosterone energises a man. As a woman is hugged and touched, oxytocins, which are calming and relaxing chemicals, are released into her system.

Connect with each other as you arrive home with a de-stressing hug and take a minute to reconnect with each other's world.

Plan meaningful conversations

Positive conversations are like seeds that germinate to create belief and expectation. So what you plant is what will grow.

Engage in spirited discussions, without putting each other down. Enjoy the cut and thrust of your differing opinions and perspectives. Think of each other as a valuable resource for ideas.

People in happy marriages often talk about feeling safe. Safe to share their deepest thoughts and secrets. Safe emotionally. There are

hot tip ✓

If you want to get the best from a man make sure that you ask him in a way that will maximise your chances of a positive response. Men tend to tune out chit-chat so get to the point.

Ask for one thing at a time and avoid the laundry list approach.

Don't phrase questions with 'Can you . . .' or 'Could you . . . ?' – they tend to irritate men because they are indirect. Try more straightforward requests like 'Will you . . .?' or 'Would you . . .?' and calmly repeat the request without a whine or pleading.

Get his attention with praise. Focus on what he did that you appreciated, not on his character. He is likely to be suspicious if you link his character to a job. Cushion a request to do something different with praise. For example, 'Thank you for fixing that gate. It is a real load off my mind to know that it works. Unfortunately three-year-old Jamie next door can still reach it. Would you readjust it for him? I'm so grateful for your expertise so that we don't have to get a builder in to do job like that.'

boundaries on words, so that even in arguments they refuse to allow themselves the indulgence of ripping the other's self-worth apart.

Co-dependence

While intimacy is the key to any successful relationship, you will be well aware that you are closer to your partner in some areas than in others. Intimacy does not mean crushing each other's individuality — but true intimacy will enrich your life.

There are extremes that will put pressure on communication

and intimacy. Plugging in to another person for our identity and emotional survival will suffocate and tyrannise a relationship with demands.

Human beings cannot sustain that level of being plugged into another. Accept who you are and look at how you can grow in the areas that you are looking to your husband or wife to complete for you. A partnership is two interdependent human beings, not co-dependent victims trying to force each other to meet needs.

But allow the acceptance that your marriage gives you to develop real emotional intimacy. That means sharing your innermost feelings with your partner — your emotional pains and delights; your hopes and ambitions and deep-felt fears; your longings, your frustrations and your failures. It is said that within each of us is a 'spectator listener', who is aware if the other person is listening to them in depth. If that 'spectator listener' signals that they are not being heard as a person then they are likely to not fully reveal themselves. We withhold or water down what we really think and feel because we know that no one is really listening.

Idealisation and then disappointment were illustrated in the story of John Newton, who wrote the well-known song *Amazing Grace*. John Newton was a notorious slave trader working the coast of Africa in the 1800s. After a series of events that caused him to reflect deeply on his life, he converted to Christianity, renounced his sordid past and looked towards an entirely different type of future. He returned to England and sought out a childhood sweetheart, Polly Catlett, who, as good luck would have it, was still single. As John Pollock wrote in his biography of Newton, *Amazing Grace*, 'He found Polly a young woman of poise and charm and good nature, with the same simplicity which had captured his heart long ago . . . In Polly he saw innocence and gentleness in a

Action lab

Learn to ask the sort of questions that will keep you connected. Try these!

- *Do I behave towards you as though you were the most important person in my life?*
- *When I am with you in the presence of others, do I act towards you in ways that communicate to others that our relationship is really important to me?*
- *Is there something that I am not doing that I could do to make you feel more loved?*

world which, for him as a slave trader, was filled with deceit and violence. She was pure: only for Polly could he conquer lust. Her love would be his calm harbour where his restless, homeless spirit could anchor, to enjoy again the sunshine which had gone out of his life when his mother died.'

If that were a Mills & Boon story, there is every chance that John Newton would have lived happily ever after, with Polly's love his constant source of healing for his past and sustenance for his future. However, because this was real life, that did not happen. What did happen was entirely different from what he had imagined. But for their long-term happiness and interdependence, it was by far the best thing that could have taken place. Disappointment set in, as it tends to when we set up idealisations. John, eager for heights of emotion yet diffident and awkward around women, reacted to Polly's cautious and reserved personality. Suddenly she didn't seem to be quite the Polly of his dreams. John Pollock states that he 'passed some uncomfortable weeks. Then as he put it afterwards to Polly, "The prospect cleared up, and by quick stages I attained to that consciousness of your affection, which I would not exchange for empire and the riches of the whole globe." They fell irrecoverably in love. Her constant endearments loosened his tongue and, as he later would say, "Love cannot be ardent and intense until it becomes reciprocal."'

This observation of John Newton's may seem obvious, but it is amazing how many of us are subconsciously operating out of 'need-love'. We are oblivious, until we have some insight, into why we are not receiving the love we need. We have not 'clicked' that 'love needs to be reciprocal'. We are blinded by our own needs and neediness, and immaturity makes us want to plug into another person for survival.

Working on wholeness

It is helpful to look at what constitutes a healthy, mature adult. Healthy individuation is when we deeply acknowledge that everyone has value and significance and that our survival is not dependent on another. We cannot love another person until we are reasonably whole ourselves and understand that identity and significance issues don't lie in another human being. Until we have made friends with the fact that we all have intrinsic significance and value, we will be forever looking for a perfect partner who, we hope, will make us feel whole and then, through imposing on that relationship impossible demands, even end up losing it.

Many marriages falter when one partner is disappointed that their lover cannot meet all their expectations. They become defensive and angry, often consciously or subconsciously punishing the partner for his or her failure to live up to their dreams. These expectations may be totally unrealistic, but they still cause the person to go on the defensive, and in psychological language, take a dysfunctional position. They see their partner as a stumbling block to their happiness and consequently any comment or criticism is an attack on the root of their identity.

That sort of neediness, where we try to bully our partner into healing us and meeting all our needs, is often labelled co-dependence. Unfortunately we will never be able to love or be loved if we look for love this way. If we look for love by trying to bully our partner into meeting our needs, we will actually destroy the love that is there in the first place. And if we do succeed in manipulating our partner into meeting our needs, it will never be real love which is freely given between two loving adults. It will be something else entirely.

Always speak with love – always listen with love. Isolation is when one partner excludes the other. You may be living together but not sharing a life.

Connect regularly in little ways each day. A kiss, a gentle neck rub or a pat can ease tensions and create deep feelings of security and love between husband and wife even when surrounding circumstances are hectic.

The ultimate is to have a mate beside us who has the same goals and dreams and wants to make a difference.

Every marriage needs a plan to defeat isolation and neglect.

CHAPTER 7

Physical needs in marriage

Sex . . . has a purpose . . . to abolish isolation. Some people choose isolation. They do so not because at heart they prefer isolation but because they fear rejection and estrangement. Yet if I do not expose myself, how will I ever discover the wonders of being enfolded by and lost in another?

John White, *Eros Defiled*

Winter pyjamas – on behalf of all optically aware guys, do not wear them on your wedding night – or anytime your husband is not away on an overnight business trip.

Joey O'Connor, *Have Your Wedding Cake and Eat it Too*

Love is an act of endless forgiveness,
a tender look that becomes a habit.

Peter Ustinov

Love is meeting needs.

Physical needs for nurture and comfort

Physical contact is a powerful way to convey positive emotions and nurture your partner's spirit. *Anatomy of Love* anthropologist Helen Fisher describes why touch is so powerful. 'Human skin is like a field of grass, each blade a nerve ending so sensitive that the slightest graze can etch into the human brain a memory of the moment.'

Imagine one of those days when everything in the history of the world that could go wrong, has gone wrong. Your wife just comes off the phone from reporting to the police station that Johnny's bike has been stolen, when she finds Emma has fallen out of the treehouse and broken her arm! After sitting at the hospital for several hours waiting for Emma to have her arm X-rayed, she arrives home to find a sock has got caught in the outlet of the washing machine and the laundry is flooded!

If you arrive home and wrap her in your arms, will that make a difference? Yes, it literally will change everything. You see, that hug spurs a rise in haemoglobin, a substance in the red blood cells that transports energising oxygen throughout the body. Incredibly, your gentle touch causes a speeding heart to quiet, soaring blood pressure to drop, and severe pain to ease.

Considering its powerful impact, it is no wonder that touch is known as the 'mother of the senses'. There is simply no better way to communicate: 'You're not alone', 'You're important', 'I'm sorry', or 'I love you'.

A woman's main physical need is non-sexual touch

Hollywood hype notwithstanding, 80 per cent of a woman's physical need is non-sexual touch. We often say at our marriage seminars that a woman needs 10 non-sexual hugs a day. Most men aren't sure how that is possible, because a man lives with a challenge called testosterone. That testosterone is likely to stimulate a sexual thought as often as every five seconds! So he will probably have to learn to control his hands' urge to wander!

A young woman approached us recently at a marriage seminar and said that ever since they attended one of our marriage evenings, her husband gets up each morning and gives her 10 hugs. 'He goes one, two, three, four . . . etc. just to make sure that he has fulfilled the quota!' The humour and kindness in that action, however, is letting her know that he *heard*, and is aware of that need.

Men usually think that the obvious most pleasurable activity with their wife is sex, but in a survey several years ago in the *New York Times*, sex came twelfth for women on a list of her most pleasurable activities. In fact it was behind gardening! The top of the list for women was affection along with openness and honesty, whereas the men put sex and respect on top of their list of priorities.

Women connect sex with a far wider variety of information than just the physical, especially the quality of the relationship. Women overwhelmingly cite affection and intimacy as their reason for liking sex. When they don't have it, they miss the companionship of sex, whereas men just miss the sex. Men: if you don't take time to talk to her, dance with her sometimes, just look at her lovingly as she tells you about her day, and touch and kiss her sensually, then she is likely to feel used.

A woman needs emotional fulfilment in order to respond sexually

She needs meaningful dialogue and warmth; hugging and kissing. If you go out of your way to help your wife fulfil her daily word count by hearing her heart and asking the sort of questions that cause her to feel listened to, you'll be the man she always longed for. That sort of talking registers on her radar and makes her feel close to you.

Men and sex

Men are physiologically wired to be aroused visually and they live every day with this reality. Just as she needs conversation, he needs to physically express his love sexually. His desire for sex with his wife tends to be an expression of love and his desire to get close. And men usually want sex more than their wives do.

When men are asked about romance they usually think of sex. We often underestimate the statement that men are biological and women emotional. A man has an acute sense of sexual sight and he enjoys using it as often as possible, so when he says he likes you in that lingerie he bought you, he is expressing a genuine pleasure.

In her 2009 book *The Sex Diaries*, sex therapist Bettina Arndt addresses the topic of men's and women's biologically mismatched sexual libidos and has, to some extent, lifted the lid on previously unspoken realities of modern marriages. Based on the bedroom revelations of 98 Australian couples over six to nine months, the book has been a bestseller as well as a headline grabber.

Her message that '[i]t simply hasn't worked to have a couple's sex life hinge on the fragile, feeble female libido' is a radical idea in our post women's liberation culture, and she has received a host of negative reaction from some quarters. But her conclusions highlight, for the first time, the plight of modern men living with the reality of their biology while committing to a faithful relationship with their wives. 'The right to say "no", needs to give way to saying "yes" more often,' she suggests. Only 10 per cent of Arndt's female diarists had higher sex drives than their partners and her book is full of the anguish of the men whose wives have just lost interest. Arndt says that female libido is so fragile it is easy to find excuses not to have sex. But desire is a decision. 'Women have to make a decision to put sex back on the "to do" list because if you allow these other things to swamp your sexual interest, your relationship will be in real trouble.' Of course 'resentment is a passion killer', and an unequal share of household duties has

hot tip ✓

- Give yourself permission to show affection and touch more often. Practise meaningful touch.
- Practise kindness, gentleness, helping with chores and bringing home small gifts occasionally. A 10-second kiss connects in a romantic physical way. Don't just guess at the 10 seconds — time yourself the first time! Tell the children that Mum is allowed to be the first one to get a kiss from Dad. They are next!
- Ask your partner what they find appealing.

> Mismatched desire need not spell the end of a couple's sex life . . . women still may enjoy sex even if they don't initially crave it.

long been high on a woman's list of resentments, along with their exhaustion from kids, dinner, the shopping, homework, and so on.

However, Arndt is not totally convinced that it is solely about those things. Apparently men have tried to up their share of the housework (8 per cent since 1992), yet judging from the sex diaries it does not seem to have increased their share of sex.[5] In her chapter 'Laundry gets you laid', one of Arndt's diarists describes her husband as a domestic god, yet their libidos are still worlds apart.

'But it strikes me as being so unfair that women feel entitled to voice their complaints and demands of a relationship, yet a lot of men have at the absolute top of their wants and needs, more sex and it is being totally ignored. How can we justify simply shutting up shop or forcing a man into a life spent grovelling for sex?'

> I am totally at a loss as to what to do' writes Andrew, 41-year-old diarist, married for six years, with two children. He said he and his wife used to have sex every day, but are down to once every five or six months, 'I do love her and I think she loves me but I cannot live like a monk . . . What makes women think that halfway through the game they can change the rules to suit themselves and expect the male to take it.
>
> **Bettina Arndt,** *The Sex Diaries*

The picture Arndt gets from her male sex diarists is in large part a lament for love denied. They love their wives but desperately need the intimacy they used to have. They feel cheated.

Arndt is not saying women should have sex against their will, but suggests they heed new research that shows they may still enjoy sex, even if they didn't crave it in the first place. Arndt also states that the other side of the equation is women's guilt at their own lower sex drive.

'Understanding that male and female sex drives are different was the key to rapprochement in the bedroom. It is all about walking in each other's shoes.

'Most of the women are upset that they don't want sex. It is not a deliberate thing . . . but we have to find a way around it if we are going to have marriages lasting many years.'

Men tend to have higher testosterone levels in the morning whereas their wives' libidos tend to be more active later in the day; and men deprived of sex are much more likely to become morose and irritable.

However, women live with a monthly cycle which gives them higher energy, sex drive and even higher self-esteem at certain times of the month.

So, given these seemingly insurmountable differences, can you ever achieve real harmony with your partner?

Think of meeting needs as an act of love. When you each understand the other's needs and work towards meeting them you will become a winning team. Leading sex researchers Masters and Johnson found that those who experienced the most sexual pleasure were the partners who were trying to please each other.

Love is meeting needs, and so teaching each other what makes us feel loved will build a great loving relationship.

Challenges for women – her hormones and emotional make-up

Women have a very different emotional make-up and hormonal interior life to men. In lots of ways it is now acknowledged that women *are* their hormones.

Women cry more easily and respond emotionally and in a more nurturing way to situations and certain stimuli. Actually this 'up and downness' can be a gift. It is as if women have bigger springs than men — as in a vehicle on a rough road. It means that the bumps in life may feel bigger, but their emotional 'springs' allow them a certain resilience which helps them to negotiate those bumps.

It is often a normal part of a female hormonal cycle to feel low, depressed or emotional at times and we need to explain this to our husbands and map those times when we are likely to feel depleted, stressed or emotional. One friend confided in Mary that she suffered so badly from PMT that she did so much damage in the two weeks before her monthly period that it took her the other two weeks to repair the relationship! Learning to say to your

hot tip ✔

If you are a couple struggling with exhaustion, young children and big workloads, promise each other that one night a week is 'sex' night. Don't let this become an ongoing battle that is never resolved. A man can wait if he knows that he is promised 'on Wednesday' for instance.

As a wife, put it in your schedule and plan it as a 'night in' — perhaps a candlelit dinner after the children are in bed, so there is pleasure for you both. Do this as your 'date' night.

hot tip ✔

- Check that no harmful viruses are affecting your mental processes and have left 'cookies' that allow destructive-relationship thinking to affect your mental processes.
- Harmful viruses are usually in the realm of lust or fantasies, that create another shadowy figure in your relationship with your spouse. The old African proverb is still true. You can't stop the birds flying over your head, but you can stop them making nests in your hair. In today's culture you are exposed to all sorts of images. You have to deliberately screen what you will allow yourself to think about.

partner, 'Darling, this is not about you, I'm just feeling terrible — this is about my hormones', or something similar, can make all the difference as to whether he withdraws from you or takes you in his arms and then makes you a cup of tea!

In her book *The Female Brain*, neuro-psychiatrist Louann Brizendine argues that women have often suffered when differences between men's and women's brains have been ignored. 'When these patients tried to talk to their own doctors or psychiatrists about how their hormones were affecting their emotions they would get the brush-off.' Don't underestimate the chances that what appears to be a relationship issue can sometimes be hormonal and helped markedly by a supplement or through medical help. For women, things like anger, mood swings, irritability, lack of energy and weepiness can all be hormonal imbalances of various sorts.

Living with the cycle

In the first fortnight of a woman's menstrual cycle, levels of the hormone oestrogen are higher, which gives her a sense of well-being, enthusiasm, alertness and self-esteem. Progesterone, which has a tranquillising effect, is also present. Both these hormones become depleted in the second half of her cycle.

Oestrogen and progesterone are mind-altering chemicals, and their changing levels can influence a woman's personality and cause unpredictable, sometimes unpleasant, mood swings. When this happens, those around her often feel attacked and withdraw at the very time she needs comforting the most. The love of an understanding partner is the perfect antidote.

Men, when you see your wife suffering from the mood swings associated with her menstrual cycle, you may like to feel thankful you don't suffer in a similar way, and offer her your comfort and support.

The separation of sex from love in our media-saturated society

Are you often incredulous at the way that sex is used by every section of the media to deliver one's fantasies? Even more so now, with the explosion of reality TV and 'in your face' game shows about dating and relationships. We can't help feeling that we are devaluing for the next generation a precious component in life.

There would be few people who wouldn't acknowledge that using sex in this way is exploitive; however, an even more concerning issue is the way that overt sexuality on our TV or movie screens is linked not to tenderness but to bawdiness, to rough sex and to a lack of intimacy.

All human beings long for intimacy and faithfulness. Bringing

Action lab

The five-day surprise

- *On Tuesday leave your husband two chocolates with a note that says, 'You're sweet!'*
- *On Wednesday, two bananas with a note that says, 'Interested in some monkey business on Saturday night?'*
- *On Thursday, marshmallows and a note, 'Your love makes me light-headed'.*
- *On Friday, a piece of angel-food cake and a note from your 'angel'.*
- *On Saturday, set up the bed with candles, special music and cushions.*

sex out of the bedroom and into a voyeuristic experience may have robbed many of the real experience. Mike Mason in *The Mystery of Marriage* discusses total nakedness. 'To be naked with another person is a sort of picture of symbolic demonstration of perfect honesty, perfect trust, perfect giving and commitment and if the heart is not naked along with the body then the whole action becomes a lie and a mockery. It becomes an ennoblement in an absurd and tragic contradiction: the giving of the body but the withholding of the self.'

In the second half of the twentieth century sex has been overdone, over-portrayed and over-emphasised. We have seen it everywhere, at times cheapened and at times sentimentalised and idolised but nearly always out of the context of marriage.

This one-dimensional view of sex has the potential to set up couples for disappointment and loneliness. Even pornography is sometimes defended as legitimate within the bedroom. We suggest that this is the ultimate insult to one's partner and a form of unfaithfulness.

The lack of building intimacy before couples hop into bed together, as portrayed in the media, gives an impression that will no doubt set more and more people up for disappointment and isolation.

The way we treat each other outside the bedroom affects what happens inside the bedroom.

CHAPTER 8

A safe haven for the expression of differences, anger and conflict

The only qualification you need to be married is to be able to resolve a dispute without hurting each other. All the rest is luxury. This is the only necessity.

Dave Riddell, *School of Living Wisdom*

Arguing becomes the condition not the exception . . . until fighting becomes the language of the relationship.

Katie (Michelle Pfeiffer), *The Story of Us*

The only person who listens to both sides of the argument is the fellow in the next apartment.

Ruth Brown, in *National Enquirer*

Handling conflict is one of the greatest challenges of achieving healthy interdependence. A balance of power and the respect for each other's autonomy are things that will challenge us and draw on the best in us. They will challenge our character, our ability to compromise and our real love. They will challenge whether we really want what is best for our marriage and what is best for our partner.

If we haven't seen conflict handled well in our own parents' marriages then we may panic and regress into patterns learned in childhood. Usually those patterns involve clamming up or blowing up.

Conflict can drive a couple apart or it can be viewed as an invitation to negotiate, or an invitation to agree. Strong emotions are usually involved when conflict arises. So unless a couple has in place some rules or simple tools to negotiate with, they tend to revert to childhood ways of relating.

Blaming, shaming, blowing up or clamming up will all be options if we don't come from backgrounds where healthy conflict resolution was practised. If, in your family of origin, issues were discussed openly and put on the table rather than addressed through personal attack, then you are much more likely to be able to establish similar practices as a couple.

Catherine Booth, co-founder of the Salvation Army with her husband William, corresponded in depth with William during their

hot tip ✔

Agree together that you will not make decisions in the home that affect the other and the rest of the family without your spouse's complete agreement. If you can't come to an agreement then you could just wait. Arguments tend to be a side effect of autonomous decisions. If one or other is left out of the decision-making process, they can feel insecure, and insecurity produces instability in other areas of marriage.

List all the reasons, pro and con, for a course of action and then list all the reasons pro and con for not doing it. Then evaluate those reasons.

three-year engagement about their future life together. She wrote to him in 1855 suggesting four rules for their future married life:

1. Never to have any secrets from my husband.
2. Never to have two purses.
3. Talk out differences of opinion to secure harmony and don't try to pretend the differences don't exist.
4. Never to argue in front of the children.[6]

Although well before the emancipation of women, Catherine's common sense and sense of natural justice ensured that she put her finger on several key points of healthy partnerships and built her marriage on those foundations.

Modern psychologists would say that to argue in front of the children really does affect them negatively if there is a lot of anger and emotion in the arguing. Coming from an unhappy home herself, Catherine knew that she wanted something better for

> Think of conflict positively: as an invitation to negotiate or an invitation to agree.

her marriage and her family. Both she and William were highly opinionated and capable. She was educated; he less educated, and awkward socially, but they formed a strong bond of love and respect, building over their lifetime together an organisation that is still having an impact on society today.

And when she, at 60, discovered that she was suffering from terminal cancer, she told her husband, 'Do you know what my first thought was? It was that I regretted that I should not be here to nurse you when you came to your last hour.' As one biographer states, 'When you put together two determined people like William and Catherine, both of whom came from problem marriages, you wouldn't expect to find the love and commitment that was evidenced by the Booths. They needed each other. At times they admonished each other; or at other times, they propped each other up. The fact of the matter is, they loved each other.'

Some people regress when there is conflict. They clam up and panic. They may even run away, and they definitely don't want to talk. Others may want to loudly rehearse the frustration and pain of the situation (especially the other's sins), immediately — and in public, if that's where it arises!

Becoming defensive can become our preferred safe option because we are not just fighting about this issue; we are fighting for deeper issues about our own significance.

> Human beings can be most obnoxious when they need love and support the most.

We cannot love or be loved when we are on the defensive.

Maturity is recognising those old childhood issues that drive us, and making friends with those childhood feelings. We can then say, 'Hey darling, this isn't about you at all. This is about how I am feeling. What I just need at the moment is your support and belief in me.'

It really is OK to argue — it's a natural part of a relationship. But an argument with your partner should be a fruitful discussion — not a destructive verbal punch-up. It can be a mutual invitation to negotiate, to resolve a particular problem in an amicable way.

A first step to achieving this is to understand the very different ways in which men and women cope with stress.

Women cannot handle being shut out by their partner when difficulties arise in a relationship. They are emotionally involved and need to talk problems through. Men prefer to solve problems in their own way and often won't talk because they think it will lead to conflict.

A wife can be a huge support to her husband if he will trust her when he is stressed. Take the example of redundancy or financial pressure. This can make a man feel like a failure yet his wife is often a willing ally in working with him on solutions to get them through. She feels stressed and isolated when he won't talk. Serious trouble is looming for a relationship when one or other withdraws during an argument.

It indicates an attitude of, 'I give up, this relationship isn't worth the trouble.'

Eighty-five per cent of withdrawals from arguments are by men. Men very often don't want to talk because they think that it will

If it really does matter to your spouse . . . then let them know that it matters to you.

hot tip ✔

Practise some 'no-blame' phrases which will keep each other off the defensive. It might be as simple as using a phrase like 'You could be right' or 'This isn't working.'

lead to arguing. They often don't feel safe and they don't know what the rules are meant to be.

As we said earlier, men tend to be more adversely affected by arguments than women and are likely to 'start flooding' at much lower levels of criticism and stay in a 'flooded' state, with all the associated negative emotions, for longer.

When men feel threatened or ridiculed they need to distance themselves from the situation, while their emotions and their heart rate settle down. They may send out their 'Rottweiler' of anger to keep you off their patch, so they can avoid engaging in what they perceive will be a stressful encounter or argument.

However, few women can stand emotional distance. Therefore men need the words to let their wife know that they need this time-out, without her feeling rejected; as well as the words to help begin the process of negotiation. Something like, 'I need time to think' or 'I want to talk but not now, can we talk after tea?' Unresolved conflict is like a cancer which if not dealt with will silently do its destructive work until it eventually becomes inoperable.

Try different – not harder

The old saying goes that if you always do what you have always done, then you'll always get what you have always had. In fact a definition of insanity is to continue to do the same thing and hope for a different result.

Many couples put themselves on the defensive with each other and by taking that dysfunctional position with each other end up losing the love they are wanting so much. You see, you cannot love or be loved when you are on the defensive. So try getting off the defensive with each other and using some different phrases such as, 'How can we work this out in such a way that we can both live with it?' A phrase such as this offers some neutral territory to begin the process of getting off the defensive.

What if there is some truth in your partner's criticism – will it really hurt you to admit it?

The thing is that we are all longing for someone who will be an emotional foil to all our hurts and bruises, not only of the present, but of the past. We are looking for that responsiveness from them; in the same way that a mother is sensitive to her young child, we are longing for that emotional availability in our partner.

Often it is not so much that we lack the skills of negotiation — in fact many men and women can negotiate brilliantly at work, but at home revert to street fighting and childish manipulation. It is that we are on the defensive, because we have been programmed to fight for our own survival.

Often we keep doing things that don't work but have no idea how to change these reactions. We suggest you try a different way.

Unlatch a negative sequence by dropping your defences and

> There are four words that may be more important in marriage than 'Darling, I'm sorry.' They are, 'You could be right.'

using a no-blame phrase such as 'Darling, this isn't working' or 'Hey, this isn't like you — what is really going on?'

After a rocky patch in their marriages, couples have talked about how they have gained a new appreciation of their relationship by changing their style; and in so doing, their perception of their partner changes.

We may not be able to change others but we can make decisions to change our own responses, and thereby influence others.

We can become less critical and more affirming; less emotionally closed and more open in sharing; or less controlling and more vulnerable.

Use humour whenever possible

One of the main characteristics of happy relationships is that the partners can respond in a positive, non-defensive way to negative stimuli from the other.

When a relationship is stuck, it is amazing how, by taking a new position with humour or teasing, trying out new steps slowly and calmly, we can change the equation. It is amazing how we can overcome negativity by a friendly overture. It can be as simple as turning off the TV when she needs to talk or using one of our children's cute sayings. One wife says when she and her husband were arguing over the car, she poked her tongue out like she had seen their son do that morning — they both fell about laughing and realised that the confrontation was silly.

How can we work this out so we can both live with it?

The key to a healthy relationship is equality — and a balance of power, particularly during a heated discussion or argument. However, as we all know from personal experience, even the most reasoned discussion can become highly emotional and degenerate into hurtful confrontation, if one or other feels unlistened to.

These situations don't improve unless there are some ground rules. Objective ground rules help us to concentrate on the problem, to both stay on the same side against the problem and to feel safe while working through the conflict to resolution.

Many couples are stuck on the same issues, merely because they don't have the tools to get unstuck and move on and they don't have the external ground rules.

In 1998 Mary and I attended a course at Denver University run by Scott Stanley, Howard Markman and Susan Blumberg. They are the authors and co-authors of several books including *Fighting for Your Marriage* and *We Can Work it Out*. They had conducted research over several years with distressed couples and had filmed a unique series with the television programme *20/20*. In this series couples who were having terrible marital conflict volunteered to be filmed both before and after they were given a skill for working through conflict.

They explained how often couples would ring, volunteering to be part of the filming because they were experiencing unresolvable conflict. They were amazed how often these couples were able to stop the argument and then pick it up 48 hours later, when

Stay on the same side *against* the problem.

the camera crew got there! They concluded that many couples have key issues; and that they return to the same arguments over and over, because they don't have a safe way of resolving their differences and moving on.

This trio of university researchers have developed a simple tool for working through differences. Below is our adapted version of that tool.

If you are reading this book and would like better ways of resolving conflict in your relationship than you currently have, then we strongly encourage you to try it out. We know couples who have come to one of our marriage evenings separately, on the brink of divorce, and met afterwards at a hotel or somewhere similar to talk and use this idea, and before the evening was over had reconciled.

It may appear too simple an idea and you may even feel foolish

hot tip ✔

- Practise non-defensive ways of responding, which are different from your responses in the past.
- Next time you feel criticised, try to take a different position.
- Try getting off the defensive and simply agreeing with your spouse, then asking for more love and help in solving the problem.
- Your responses could be: 'I see your point.' 'How can we solve this in such a way that we can both live with it?' 'What do you think would be the best way for me to handle my emotions, when I hit that trigger in future?'

hot tip ✔

- It is always best to negotiate early so that small issues are dealt with before you get stuck in a heavy-duty conflict situation.
- Try a weekly 'couple meeting' (this is not a date night). Knowing that this is going to happen takes so much pressure off as you know that you can address one thing each that you feel needs talking about. Make it a regular time, perhaps outside your home in a café or picnic spot, when you are not tired or stressed. Always begin by reaffirming your love and commitment to each other first before you address any negatives.
- Have demilitarised zones in your marriage. These are time frames when you will not bring up issues and you both know there won't be any pressure to do so.

initially working through the sequence of steps — yet it is an amazingly powerful way of very quickly resolving even the worst issues between couples.

Think of it like this. If you have never been good at conflict resolution or listening to each other's perspective, then the patterns you have developed will be hard to break out of. Ian was a bad stutterer as a child and teenager and it has been a lifelong battle for him to speak on the telephone and even 'one on one' if there is a lot of noise in the room.

By far the most helpful course he has attended for stutterers is one called 'Smooth Speech'. In this course, they work with the participants to slow their speech right down until they reach a level of slow speaking at which their stutter disappears. Then the instructors will gradually help their pupils to bring their speech back

Action lab

- *What need does your spouse have that you could meet today? A car wash, assistance with the housework, actioning an errand that has been shelved? Choose a gesture that says, 'I cherish you, I respect you.'*

up to a more normal pace. Of course it takes practice afterwards to break habits of a lifetime, but it is amazing how even the worst stutterers can speak smoothly at this slow rhythm. In the same way as you slow down the way you address conflict, by using the steps in this method, you will be amazed how the issues can be resolved and you may find yourselves listening to each other in a truly fresh way.

In fact on our way home from that trip to Denver, we decided to talk about an issue we had both never felt really 'heard' over. Looking for something to use we took out of the seat pocket in front of us an Air New Zealand 'airsick' bag and we used it as our 'floor'. We were both secure enough to launch into a discussion in public, about a topic which had at times been emotional for us and laced with misunderstandings. The reason was that we knew there were rules and those rules kept us safe from falling back into defensiveness or attacking each other.

Sometimes couples will just decide to avoid certain subjects because they know they will be too painful to allow them to surface. This method takes away those sorts of reservations and means you can go there, even into what has been in the past rocky territory, because you know that there will be a way through.

Using 'the floor' to safely negotiate tricky territory

The key to this method is '**the floor**'. The overriding rule is that the person holding **the floor** — has the floor. The other person must listen and not interrupt until the process of listening and repeating back is finished and **the floor** is handed over. There are rules for the speaker and rules for the listener.

The floor can be a piece of card, the salt shaker, or any object that you decide on. In our family it has become the pepper mill. However, at dinner parties we have used this method to conduct lively discussions with several people, and have used anything from a serviette to a wine bottle!

The rules also forbid mind-reading or rebutting. No one is allowed to say 'Don't be ridiculous', 'What a lot of rubbish', or any other statement that rebuts the feelings or observations of the other. Similarly no one is allowed to assume what the other is thinking. Use this method for arguments or when you can't agree.

Step One: Get the feelings out

- *Hold* **the floor** *and express your feelings and what you need. (Remember, no interrupting from the listener.) Share feelings only, not judgements or solutions.*
- *Hold on to* **the floor** *while your partner repeats back what he/she thinks they have heard you say. You hold onto* **the floor** *until you are sure that your partner has heard you. (Keep your statements brief — the listener could use lines such as 'It sounds like you . . .', or 'It seems that . . .').*
- *When you are sure that your feelings have been heard and acknowledged, then hand over* **the floor** *to your partner and he/she may then take their turn at sharing their feelings, while you listen. Then you repeat back to them what you think they are trying to say. They then don't need to surrender* **the floor** *until they definitely feel you have heard their feelings.*

Don't rush this process. Once you have both got all your feelings out, then you can move on to step two. Many of us want to get onto the solution process before we have got all the feelings out on the table. Feelings are not always telling us the truth, and our perceptions may be askew, but we will not feel understood until we get them out. Even actually participating in this process may bring with it a huge sense of relief. Not feeling heard is often the source of your pain when issues arise between you.

Action lab

- *Don't go along with decisions you are not happy with. Agreeing for the sake of peace will always cause a resentment backlash. Resolve the ambivalence before it becomes full-blown resentment.*
- *Use the floor to express your feelings on any issue that you have felt pushed into.*

Step Two: Work on solutions

- *Each take a turn at coming up with ideas that might be solutions. No ideas are right or wrong. Treat them like balloons that you are floating in the air. Try to come up with all possible ideas, not just the ones you think will work the best. You can write these ideas down if you prefer to see them in black and white.*
- *Eliminate those ideas that you both decide won't work.*
- *Choose those ideas that might work and that you can both live with.*
- *If none of the ideas are going to work then that is OK. Agree to do some more research, maybe look for more*

information, and revisit the discussion in 24 hours.

Importantly, if one partner needs to talk, and produces **the floor** at a time when the other is so exhausted that they just can't face it, then the other must set a time within 48 hours when they agree to talk.

And if, for some reason, one of you is in overload emotionally, you can say 'stop action' and set a time to talk again within 48 hours. Stop action is not a rejection — it is so you can take 'time-out'. It just means, 'I am overloaded so I need to be able to come back more respectfully. My anger causes me to be disrespectful. You're overwhelming me.'

These are the rules and they create reassurance for both that it is possible to work through even their worst disagreements.

You don't have to finish every argument before you go to bed . . . you can agree on sorting the problem out when you are less tired — as long as you both know what the rules are! Besides, things often look better in the morning. Or if conflict arises at an inappropriate time, suggest to your partner, 'Let's talk about this when the children are asleep, or after the news.' (And stick to it.) Some couples have a 'flag' they use when they need a talk.

We need to be constantly reassessing our values and our perspective on life and deciding what really is important. Don't sweat the stuff that really is small. Sometimes arguments between partners can be as trivial as the right way to eat a boiled egg. Yet these little things become big because they are not aired or the listening and feeling part of the equation in communication is ignored.

Action lab

- *Arguments or rows over expectations tend to have two parts: what actually happened and how the other felt.*
- *For instance,* Phil came home late without phoning *is what actually happened.*
- *However, Jane's feelings are, 'He doesn't care about me/ he's hanging out with someone else.'*
- *Fights start because the two things get confused. She accuses and he defends, saying, 'I'm working hard and I don't need any more hassle. You are totally overreacting.'*
- *However, if you can keep the two parts separate, then the real issue becomes: how did the wounded party feel and what needs to happen for them to feel better?*
- *Maybe the solution will be to promise always to phone and then perhaps spend some extra time together later in the week.*

Always express your perspective on issues *honestly* and with *consideration* for the other person because these are two fundamental requirements to sustain a long-term good marriage.

If it really does matter to your spouse then let them know that it also matters to you — don't trivialise what is important to them.

Which schools your children attend, or where you go for holidays, may not be important to you, but if they are issues for your partner then make sure you take up the invitation to negotiate and to come to an agreement.

Remember accessibility and responsiveness are the qualities

that will create and maintain secure bonds.

Mary often tells of how she always knew that if she ever desperately needed me, I would be available. My staff knew that she was always able to get through to me, no matter how important the meeting or programme that I was involved in. I have many imperfections as a husband but the fact that I had created that primacy of importance of being available, she says, meant so much. In the same way I truly appreciate the many times Mary has dropped everything to be available when I needed her.

CHAPTER 9

Marriage viruses and spam

And that is what learning is. You suddenly understand something you've understood all your life, but in a new way.

Doris Lessing

The heart has reasons that reason cannot know.

Blaise Pascall

I did not try to argue as, by that time in our marriage, I knew it would be useless. Instead I thought of my favourite quote from Albert Einstein. 'Some men spend a lifetime in an attempt to comprehend the complexities of women. Others preoccupy themselves with simpler tasks such as understanding the theory of relativity.'

Sir Ranulph Fiennes, *Mad, Bad and Dangerous to Know*

If you are doing things that make each other unhappy it may not matter how hard you are working at making deposits in each other's love banks, you will be gradually eroding your capital. Just like a virus ignored on your computer, you will be corrupting all your love files. Your habits will powerfully affect the love you and your spouse have for each other — and if those things that you regularly do hurt or anger each other they will eventually contaminate your spouse's love files and rob your love banks of their romantic equity.

Caring for each other's emotional needs is not enough to maintain the feeling of love. Dr Willard Harley, author of *Fall in Love, Stay in Love*, talks about how over years of working with couples he is fascinated by human instincts and the difficulty most people have in overriding them. We bring into our marriages habits which are not only often stupid and abusive but which just don't work, yet which we continue to practise because we don't actually see the danger of these ways of operation. 'You must also protect your spouse from habits that cause his or her unhappiness. Neither you nor your spouse married to hurt each other yet if you are not careful you can become the greatest source of each other's unhappiness and if you don't make a special effort to protect each other from your own selfish instincts and habits, it's inevitable.'

Work differently – not harder – at the way you try to integrate each other's needs and wants.

Passion-killing viruses that drain your love banks

Viruses take many forms. They may be selfish demands, annoying habits, disrespectful judgements, angry outbursts, or doing your own thing.

Some of these are thoughtless immature ways of acting; others are deliberate behaviour designed to manipulate the other into doing what we want. Ways of getting what you want may be instinctive yet thoughtless. As we mentioned earlier, it is amazing how spouses tend to downgrade their behaviour once they are married. When you are courting you tend to be thoughtful and considerate; and you would probably never have ended up together if you had shown the selfish habits that we sometimes give ourselves permission to resort to once we marry and set up house together.

What form do they take?

When a spouse doesn't get what they want they may resort to a *demand*. I don't care what you feel — do it or else. If that doesn't work then we may try *disrespectful judgement:* 'If you were not so selfish', and when that fails, we may use an *angry outburst* to try to bully the other into action: 'It's always your way or no way, isn't it!'

Why they don't work

Of course none of these strategies actually work or get you what you want because they tend to create resentment or resistance. They nearly always make the other person less caring and responsive and cause him or her to withdraw from you, thus creating distance not closeness.

When you indulge in this sort of behaviour you not only don't get what you need or want but you also destroy the love your spouse has for you. You cause hurt, unhappiness and therefore major withdrawals from your spouse's love bank. We have several times mentioned the term 'sensitively responsive' to each other

> A lack of empathy for the other's feelings causes us to act in ways that corrupt the files of the good deposits we once made.

as being the key to creating secure bonds. You see, it is a lack of empathy for the other's feelings that causes us to go ahead and act in these uncaring ways. And days, weeks and months of this behaviour will corrupt the content of the love bank no matter how much you once deposited.

Annoying habits, independent behaviour and dishonesty are the other three categories of virus that Dr Harley associates with killing passion and sensitivity and preventing marital compatibility.

These big viruses need positive action and a united plan to eliminate them. Their insidious destructive power is that they communicate thoughtlessness and lack of consideration of the other's feelings. We often minimise our own responsibility for a bad habit that annoys or upsets our partner, by saying something like, 'Why make a court case out of it — it's no big deal!' But if the way you eat granny smith apples in bed at night or the fact that you pick your teeth in public upsets or annoys your partner, brushing off their requests shows a lack of empathy and is refusing to acknowledge that the other's feelings have any value.

Doing your own thing without considering the other isolates your partner in a hurtful way. If you act, after marriage, as if you are an independent singleton and fail to communicate if you are going to be home late or are bringing home a colleague for coffee, then you are acting disrespectfully. If you decide to sign up for a sport or a weekend away without consulting the other, you invite isolation and distance because you are acting as if the other doesn't exist.

Finally, dishonesty is like a wall that grows between two

partners. Dishonesty is like a cancer because secrets and lies subtly poison a relationship even if they are never found out. It is an old saying that a family is as sick as its secrets, and that is true of a marriage. It is true in the little things, like an impulse purchase or a delay in arriving home because of lingering unnecessarily with colleagues over a drink, as well as in really big things like infidelity.

An extreme example comes to mind from the novel *The Memory Keeper's Daughter* by Kim Edwards. A young couple — very much in love — arrive at the hospital during a blizzard, for the imminent birth of their first-born twins. The young husband is also a doctor and is, through circumstances, the only one in the hospital that night able to deliver the twin babies. The boy is healthy but the little girl is a Down syndrome child. In an instant decision, the husband, remembering the pain of his own childhood growing up with a sickly sister, hands the tiny baby to his nurse and asks for her to be taken to an orphanage. Thinking he is saving his wife from pain, he tells her the girl baby has died at birth. The rest of the story is the saga of how subtly this huge lie between them,

Action lab

Peace talks

- *Plan peace talks regularly, when you each are allowed to raise one issue that you feel is becoming a negative in your relationship.*
- *Include in the rules the essential that you begin with the phrase 'Darling, you know that I love you and am committed to you.'*
- *Hold your peace talks in a favourite café or similar.*
- *Finish with a positive affirmation of each other.*

Some rules you set together might be:

- We will always ring home if delayed.
- We will never go to bed angry.
- We will never use sex as a bargaining chip.
- We will never make important decisions affecting the other without consultation.
- We will never criticise each other in public.
- We will eat together whenever possible.

unspoken and unknown, unravels and destroys their marriage, along with all the promise of their earlier happiness.

Disempowering the 'biggies' in the virus family

Virus No. 1: Doing your own thing

We talked in an earlier chapter about 'building' a life together. And part of that building a life is deciding on a 'we culture'. If you have put in place some principles that you both want to adhere to in your life together, then you are both much more able and likely to move in your head from the 'life of an individual' to one of a 'member of a partnership'; a life of caring for each other and a life of caring about each other. If you know what are the bottom lines or the railway tracks on which you both want your marriage to run, you will be on a good foundation for success. You need to ask yourselves, 'What will we agree on that we both understand as the "secure runway" on which we will aim to land?' Some couples never actually have this discussion and so are constantly living with expectations that the other may never have agreed to or thought of. An agreement together of what will be your 'we culture' lets you know when you are off course and will give you signals from

hot tip ✓

- Be deliberate about saying one thing each day that honours your spouse.
- Practise the notion that you will always speak with love and always listen with love.
- Remind yourself every day why you fell in love with this person.

the 'beacons' you have established, to get back to that marriage landing pad, as it were. A 'we culture' agreement also helps you to recognise when the other is showing real consideration and love. For instance if you have agreed to do the Saturday morning clean-up together, and one is busy or stressed and the other offers to do it on their own — then it will be seen gratefully as an act of love by the other, not just taken for granted.

Never come or go without greeting your spouse. The 'we culture' is the shared vision of the one life that the two of you want to create together because you are committed to each other. A 'we culture' is the intimate intertwining of personalities that makes your relationship a unique, vibrant experience with a life of its own.

The sense of being a couple is what consolidates a relationship, particularly marriage. 'We-ness' gives your relationship its staying power in the face of life's inevitable frustrations and the temptation to run away or stray. It also gives you and your partner the sense that the two of you constitute a 'sovereign country' in which you make the rules.

Your marriage is a relationship that commands loyalty and is worth defending, which means you will necessarily need to relinquish some autonomy. You will more and more make judgements on what is best for your partner and for your relationship as you learn to identify with each other and your marriage.

Virus No. 2: Disrespectful speech

Disrespectful speech reflects a lack of empathy for the effect that words and accusations have on the other. By not honouring the other's opinions or actions as valid we minimise the other's worth and are not honouring them as a person whom we love, or honouring the balance of power in the relationship. If we take no responsibility for the effect of our words then we are effectively moving into the area of domination and control of the other.

Educate each other on verbal interactions that hurt the other. You may use a phrase like, 'Hey, that wasn't a "no-blame" phrase!' Or 'Darling, I know you are under stress but I am your best friend. It hurts me when you are rude like that.' Or 'When you make jokes about me in front of others, I know that you think it is harmless, but it hurts me deeply. I feel ridiculed and disrespected.'

Always speak with love – always listen with love.

Ask forgiveness each day for anything that may have hurt the other. Create rituals that will make this easier. Like the cup of tea in bed each day, or saying the Lord's Prayer together or sharing three things as a family around the dinner table that you are thankful for. A thankful attitude causes you to think about all the good things about each other, and makes you more open to listening to what is beginning to hurt.

hot tip ✔

Verbal abuse can be driven by a need to control or stay on top, arising from the fear that one must not allow another to comment or criticise, in case that criticism turns out to be true. Often, inside a person who is verbally abusive and blaming of the other, is a little boy or girl who has low self-esteem and is desperately trying to prove their own worth — they are trying to bolster their self-esteem by putting the other down. Verbal abusers have an unconscious need to be seen as perfect.

You are likely to need objective help from a counsellor if you find yourself living with a constant bombardment of verbal bombs and grenades designed to punish you.

A marriage can be turned around with the right help — but it must begin with the realisation that the abuser has emotional needs (which can be met), but that the behaviour will not be indulged. Loving solutions include affirming the emotional need, but rejecting the behaviour. We do not help an abuser by accepting his or her destructive ways of trying to meet those needs.

(You can read more on this in *Loving Solutions* by Gary Chapman.)

Virus No. 3: Dishonesty

It may sound unrealistic but honesty must be held as the highest value in your marriage. Unfortunately many couples think that by not telling each other certain things they may save the other some pain or that some things are just best not shared. But dishonesty makes major withdrawals from your love banks. Honesty is one of the highest emotional needs that we have in marriage. You cannot build love and stay in love without it and honesty is the

> Reveal to your spouse as much information about yourself as you know – your thoughts, feelings, habits, likes, dislikes, personal history, daily activities, and plans for the future.
>
> **Dr Harley's Policy of Radical Honesty**

only way that you will ever get to really understand each other. Unfortunately many couples guess at what the other wants and through this 'hit and miss' way of trying to make the other happy actually create their own unhappiness. In other words it might not be through lack of trying that we end up corrupting a love file, but through ignorance of what the other really wants. How often have you heard wives tell jokes about the presents their husbands buy them year after year, but don't want to tell the husband that they would like something else, because they don't want to hurt his feelings. Think of it this way — if you knew your husband was telling jokes about *your* choice of presents (even in a mildly indulgent way) at the office, you would be humiliated and wish that he had told you.

Honesty will not only bring you closer together but it will prevent the growth of destructive habits. Dr Willard Harley has developed what he calls a policy of radical honesty. He believes that it may sound radical in our current society but that we lose so much if we settle for less. Dishonesty misses the opportunity to learn how to express both our positive and negative feelings, and to affirm each other when we 'hear' and respond in a different way the next time. Dr Harley's policy of radical honesty has four parts: emotional honesty, historical honesty, current honesty and future honesty. He says, 'What makes your marriage successful is your willingness and ability to accommodate each other's feelings.'

Spam attachments you bring in from your past

Many of the issues we have talked about in this chapter have their roots in our family backgrounds and early life-defining experiences. Often a behavioural pattern is not about the other person at all but an overreaction from the past, that comes out of a childish conclusion or lie the individual has taken on board about themselves.

Invisible suitcases at your marriage ceremony

When we stand at the altar on our wedding day, we stand there in a beautiful gown and a smart suit. However, what no one else sees is the two invisible suitcases we are about to lug into our marriage with us.

Only in a meaningful relationship can you truly know yourself because every belief, attitude or assumption that you hold — good or bad — comes under the microscope and the truths that are revealed can sometimes be comforting — and often discomforting.

Whenever you sense an overreaction by either you or your partner, look for the 'misbelief' underneath. It may have to be unpacked from that invisible suitcase and examined.

hot tip ✔

ASK EACH OTHER:

- 'What do you think are my biggest strengths? What strengths do you think I bring to our marriage/you bring to our marriage?'
- What is one thing you would like me to do for you?

Whenever you sense an overreaction by either you or your partner, look for the 'misbelief' underneath.

Handling the baggage

We all arrive in a relationship carrying psychological baggage bestowed on us by our family — by our mother, our father, our siblings and early experiences. We are, of course, largely the product of our own decisions in life, but there is no escaping the powerful influence our family has on us in our formative years. It has been said that we overlay the map of reality with the map of our childhood conclusions. Very often it takes an outside objective person to show us if some of those childhood conclusions were faulty.

Marriage is the laboratory in which any faulty perceptions will surface. Clearly, we need to unpack our childhood baggage and decide what is worth keeping and what must be thrown out.

> Identify the fears, prejudices and any false expectations you bring from your childhood – they distort your perception of your partner.
>
> **Dave Riddell,** School of Living Wisdom

Much of the baggage we carry is welcome: it's that trunk packed with happy memories and good influences that we are glad are ours. Some of the other baggage is less easy to lug around: regrets and guilt, relationships that have soured, bad memories, maybe even physical abuse. However, the bad things that have happened to us can, when interpreted with the benefit of maturity, be used for our own good. They often send us searching for the

Feel the feeling

Reflect on the following situations. Then share your feelings with each other, taking turns in answering first.

How do I feel when

- you smile at me?
- you reach out and touch me?
- you interrupt me?
- I think I have hurt your feelings?
- you surprise me with something nice?
- you show me you appreciate me?
- I make a mistake and you point it out?
- you are holding me tight?
- you give me a compliment?
- I think you are judging me?
- you make a sacrifice for me?
- others notice how close we are?
- you tell me you love me?
- you appear to be annoyed with me?
- I am buying a gift for you?
- I can't make you understand?
- you frown at me?
- you are too hard on yourself?
- you are upset and begin to cry?
- you are sick?
- you ask me to help you?
- you make me laugh?
- you become angry with me?
- you tell me you are proud of me?

insights we need. And at the root of it all tends to be the instinctive defence of our own value and worth. Isn't it true that, for so many of us, our strongest reactions are about our own significance and worth? An overreaction to a comment from our spouse may be triggered by an echo from the past. We may be fighting for a dignity issue that may have happened years ago, such as a school teacher telling us we would never amount to anything or a parent blaming us unfairly.

Sometimes those experiences just need to be reinterpreted, from a loving adult's point of view. Then, when the truth is substituted for those childish conclusions, just like sorting your documents, the misbeliefs can be named and neatly filed. The truth then acts as an anti-spam filter in your 'hard drive of wisdom' protecting you from those echoes from the past, and allowing you to integrate your past into your mature experience.

Cleaning out the spam

So, how do you sort out your psychological 'baggage'? This is simpler than it may seem — label it. Some is well worth keeping. Toss the rest. Learn to make the distinction.

The most potent and enduring legacy from your upbringing is the hard drive of beliefs you hold. We all have beliefs about our attractiveness, our intelligence and our personality that were shaped by incidents in our past which we may or may not remember.

During our formative years, the behaviour of our parents, relatives and family friends strongly influenced our ideas about our own value and worth as well as about how men and women relate to each other. Unfortunately many of the beliefs we accepted as gospel and carried into later life are wrong.

> Your actions come out of your feelings. Your feelings come out of what you are telling yourself. What you are telling yourself comes out of what you believe.

Wrong beliefs are usually at the heart of our wrong reactions

We think our perception of the world is the truth, but it may be that our life experience has warped that perception, and we need to re-examine what we believe to be true. Experiences from our childhood skew the true north of our map of life.

> We see the world, as a result of our experience of it, as a map. Sometimes this map is skewed by our misbeliefs and misinterpreted experiences.
>
> **Dr M Scott Peck,** *The Road Less Travelled*

Wrong beliefs can be ideas such as ‘No one listens to me’, ‘I am not loveable’, ‘I've got to fix everything’, and they will eat away at you and blight every relationship you have.

Beliefs like these and others, such as ‘My self-esteem is in my partner's hands’, ‘My husband's love is conditional on my performance’, or ‘I will never come up to my wife's expectations, so why bother?’ will lie under the surface like a submarine, coming up to do their damage when you feel vulnerable and preventing you from connecting effectively with your spouse.

What to do with a misbelief

The way to handle a misbelief is to first of all *trace it*. You will know if you have a misbelief when you overreact to something that happens, out of proportion to the incident. Then we need to *face it*. Have a good look at why you believe this wrong conclusion. Where did it come from? Is it true? And then finally *replace it* with the objective truth. You may need a friend or counsellor to help you find the antidote to a misbelief. Or you may be able to work it through yourself.

Mary and I often joke that I unwittingly married a criminal — because at three years of age Mary truanted from kindergarten, on and off for several weeks. As the middle child in a family of six, with two babies at home, she was sent to kindergarten on her third birthday. After a week or two of seemingly happily waving off her mother each morning and heading for kindergarten a mile or so up the road, she was delivered home by a neighbour who had found her an hour later playing in the bus stop. In those days, with most of the parents home and a neighbourhood that kept an eye on each other's children, it was very safe to allow children to walk this distance. After several incidents of not turning up at kindergarten and being randomly found in various locations (including looking at the dolls in the window of the local toy shop) by her mother and a neighbour, her loving but strict parents decided to do something about it. She was firmly spanked and then they arranged for one of the teachers, who walked past the gate of Mary's home on her way to work each morning, to pick her up and take her. Assuming that the reason she didn't like attending kindergarten was the long distance that she had to walk on her own, the parents managed the situation as they saw fit. However, no one at any point asked this three-year-old why she didn't want to go to kindergarten. There was a reason, known very clearly to the child herself. It was because there was a group of boys at this kindergarten who ganged up and pushed the new pupils down the slide whenever the younger ones tried to have a turn. Her

Remember – the chief thief of your good communication may be the misbelief beneath.

childish solution was to go somewhere else during kindy time and then go home when she saw the other children leaving for home.

Although this seems a small incident, it was life-defining for Mary in that, at three years old, she drew the conclusion that 'No one listens to me'. She grew up in this large, and generally very happy, family with the subconscious belief that 'No one listens to me'.

This misbelief affected many aspects of life for her, especially in the area of making a case or communicating her needs and feelings. 'No one listens to me' coloured her communication and, when she eventually married, this message became a self-fulfilling prophecy.

It was like this underlying saboteur causing her to panic if she felt unheard.

As an adult, because of the issues it caused in our marriage, with the help of a perceptive counsellor, she was able to see what was going on and to replace that belief with one that was true.

She was able to tell herself that it was OK if everyone didn't listen. Her special friends did, her children did, the local dairy owner did, and gradually the panic went out of the communication for her in our marriage also. Together we decided on a weekly date. I learned the art of questioning, giving her safe communicating time, and meeting her need to be listened to.

This one insight has had huge implications and offered great freedom for us both as a couple.

We will briefly tell you how I also brought into our marriage a belief from my childhood, which created an interface with Mary's childhood misbelief, that hijacked and corrupted many interactions in our early days.

As we mentioned earlier, I developed a stutter at the age of six, and struggled for many years with this impediment. At about seven years of age I overheard my parents discussing my stammer and how they were at a loss to know what to do — especially when it caused embarrassment for them. They were very loving parents and would not have wanted that message to be absorbed by me but again, through my imperfect childish observations, I interpreted the overheard conversation as a rejection of me. I realise that, at that point, I probably took on board the false conclusion that I was 'not good enough'. Within the context of marriage this presented a huge challenge and caused me to avoid, at all costs, any sort of personal sharing of feelings that felt to me like criticism.

We share these personal stories because we want others to know that there is real help for what may seem like unsolvable issues. We could hardly believe how, after struggling in our marriage with recurring issues over misread communication and misunderstood motives, how simple and almost instant the solution was when we found it. We want others to know that it can be that simple.

I was able to tell myself that everyone has value and worth and Mary learned to affirm my personhood and meet the emotional need under that wrong belief. Remember that the chief thief is the misbelief beneath. Understanding your own and your partner's misbeliefs will revolutionise your relationship.

For example this may be how a person is thinking: 'My state of mind is determined by my environment.'

Trace it: 'I grew up in a dysfunctional family and therefore I am destined for failure in relationships.'

Face it: 'My environment may influence, but it need not dictate, my choices.'

Replace it: 'Plenty of great people have come from bad backgrounds and overcome them with their own good choices. I am responsible for my own attitude. I can focus on the positive in my situation.'

Anger – the mega virus

Many of the biggest problems in relationships are related not just to poor communication, but to the inability to handle and process anger.

For most of us, a natural response to criticism is to bite back, but anger rarely solves anything. It pushes people away and drains your partner's love bank. Yet peace for peace's sake is never a healthy option, because it opens the way for one partner to be a bulldozer and the other a doormat.

Expressing anger is not a bad thing per se — it releases tensions and highlights problems. But you must know what to do with it; how to express it in an appropriate way so you don't dump it onto your partner, or infect your children with the anger bug. What may be a release for you may leave your family squashed and shell-shocked.

Work against the anger not against each other. Trace the root of your anger and disempower it.

When someone uses anger to keep you off their patch as it were, or you find your anger spilling over inappropriately onto others, then you need to look at where this anger is coming from. It may come from poor self-esteem or a childhood where you used anger to fend off accusations and blame. If anger has become a life habit it will

Peace for peace's sake is never a healthy option . . . it opens the way for one partner to be a bulldozer and the other a doormat.

infect your children and spoil your relationships. You need to get help if this is an issue for you.

It is amazing how easily, though, you can become less angry with a bit of thought. Anger or frustration tends to be the difference between your expectations and what is happening in reality. So you need to ask yourself how important this really is.

You can actually downgrade your anger by asking yourself, is this a disaster, or is it just disappointing?

Think of how different a circumstance might look if you saw it through the eyes of the famous Con the Fruiterer from the 1980s Australian television comedy series *The Comedy Company.* His set answer for every crisis that came his way was 'Aw . . . doesn't matter!'

Often, looking back, I made big issues of things that really didn't matter; like the fact that I couldn't find the mail when I first came home or I couldn't find a sock. I was allowing my self-talk to tell me that these things deserved my frustration levels. There were usually plenty of socks in my drawer; it was just that I couldn't find my favourite ones. (The mail was usually bills and newsletters, so they definitely weren't more important than my relationship with the family — yet I treated them as if they were!) None of these things were disasters; they were just disappointing. When I learned to downgrade the underlying belief, my frustration and anger subsided.

It is essential that partners come to an agreement on how they will manage anger in their home.

> A man who has not passed through the inferno of his passions has never overcome them.
>
> **Carl Gustav Jung,** *Memories, Dreams, Reflections*

Anna was in great distress through the struggles she and her new husband were experiencing. She knew that her anger, which since she married had seemed to explode like a volcano inside her, was constantly spilling out inappropriately onto her husband. He was bewildered by her overreactions to just about everything and started to feel that no matter what the situation, he would always be the scapegoat. He felt the sting of her anger and started to feel that she would always blame him for everything that went wrong. Subsequently he found himself closing down on her which, in turn, seemed to fuel the anger within her even more.

hot tip ✔

I often tell parents that dads are great at the parenting thing because they believe in the three Rs:

- rules
- routines
- ridiculousness.

When it comes to managing anger, I have found the three Rs have worked for me. So now when I get angry:

- My rule is to count to 10
- My routine is to get out of the situation
- My ridiculousness is I act out in my mind, 'Con the Fruiterer' from TV's *The Comedy Company*: 'It doesn't matter!'

Establish an Anger Control Contract

- Step 1: We agree to acknowledge our anger to each other as soon as we become aware of it.
- Step 2: We renounce the right to vent anger at each other. It's OK to say something like 'I'm feeling angry about – but you know I'm not going to attack you'. The other person then does not have to go on the defensive.
- Step 3: We will ask for each other's help in dealing with the anger that develops. If your partner is angry with you and appeals for your help to clear up the problem, it is very much in your interest to respond positively. Form a coalition against anger. Say, 'Our contract commits us to working on each anger situation that develops between us until we clear it up.'

Thinking that there was little hope for their marriage this young couple sought help from a counsellor. The insights that the counsellor gave them were enlightening. They learned more about how complicated we can be and about what was really going on for Anna when her husband tried to address an issue with her. In looking for what was behind the anger and where it was really coming from, they were able to trace it to an incident in Anna's childhood. Her father, an alcoholic and angry, unreasonable man, was driving Anna to school one morning when he had an accident. He blamed six-year-old Anna for distracting him and therefore causing the accident. At six years old Anna knew that the accident was not her fault and her young sense of right and wrong was violated. She went on the defensive as that young child, subconsciously sensing that adults are likely to blame you for their own mistakes, and using anger to defend herself before she could be pronounced guilty.

This couple decided to address this childhood misbelief by returning to the actual spot where the accident happened. Together they were able to talk about the incident and reinterpret the situation as a loving parent would for their six-year-old. Anna was able to tell herself that this accident was not about her, but about her panicky, alcoholic father who lashed out in anger at her because she happened to be there.

Anna found that experience to be truly freeing. She said that it was as if the 'boil' of her anger had been lanced. She still had to work on the negative patterns that she had built up, but together as a couple they were able to work against the anger, not against each other.

Refraining from judging your partner is another way of letting go of frustrations and experiencing love in the fullest sense. When you learn to accept your partner for what they are and not want to change them, you will also accept yourself.

Get to know yourself; to understand your faults. And remember the adage: 'Don't accept your dog's admiration as conclusive!'

Empathy test

How empathetic are you to each other?

1. I can name my spouse's best friends.
2. I know the stresses my spouse is facing.
3. I know the names of people who have been irritating my spouse.
4. I am aware of some of my spouse's life-dreams.
5. I know my spouse's basic philosophy of life.
6. I know the relatives my spouse likes least.
7. My spouse knows me well.
8. When we are apart, I think fondly of him/her.
9. I often touch or kiss my spouse affectionately.
10. My spouse respects me.
11. My spouse appreciates the things I do in our relationship.
12. At the end of each day my spouse is glad to see me.
13. We love talking together.
14. There is lots of give and take. (We both have influence in our discussions.)
15. We are respectful to each other, even when we disagree.
16. We generally mesh well on basic values and goals in life.

CHAPTER 10

Great partnerships

We two form a multitude. **Ovid**

The reason that husbands and wives don't understand each other, they are from opposite sexes.

Dorothy Dix

What do we live for, if it is not to make life less difficult for each other?

George Eliot, *Middlemarch*

Why we need each other

Men and women each have great strengths and these strengths when put together form great partnerships. Great partnerships recognise that the two together are stronger than one on their own and that the combined wisdom and nuances that each brings to the partnership are a gift to both. They recognise that each has something to learn from the other, as well as something they can teach the other. How wonderful to be able to come home to talk something over with someone who has a different or more objective view, who has your best interests at heart and who can also contribute their wisdom and perspective on a situation. We have talked about how our past experiences and relationships can colour our interpretation of the other's 'contribution'; taking a comment as a criticism because of those lenses from our past, or overreacting to a circumstance. Consequently, once we have looked at some of our 'baggage' or the viruses that have corrupted our files in the past, and put in their place some healthy 'truths' or virus scanners, we will be free from echoes of past experiences. We will have a much better chance of taking the goodwill of our spouse at face value and of working together to build the life of our dreams.

Melding these differences for the strength of your partnership often begins with valuing those differences. Understanding more about your partner's 'wiring' and genetic make-up can help you love and accept the best in him or her.

We also have different personalities and different ways that we like to give and receive love. It is amazing how just a small insight into these differences — and recognising that your partner is not personally trying to make your life frustrating but is wired that way — may make you laugh and may also make all the difference about how you view your life.

Men and women are the same – but different

Since the 1980s the politically correct view has been that there are no real differences between men and women. On the positive side this has helped women to gain the equality they deserve. But there is also a negative aspect to this view — the belief that equality = sameness. Such an equation is a formula for disaster in a relationship. The fact is, men and women think, feel and behave very differently. So what do we offer each other?

Why men are so valuable in relationships

Men have a great ability to get things done. They love to conquer problems. A man can achieve just about anything if he has confidence in a plan and the people involved. He has a capacity for supreme loyalty to those who believe in him and will rise to the good expectations of an affirming wife.

John Eldridge in his book *Wild at Heart: Discovering the Secret of a Man's Soul* explains how every man deep in his heart longs for three things: a battle to fight, an adventure to live and a heroine to rescue. You can see this in the sort of movies he enjoys and the recreational pursuits that men tend to engage in. It is not hard to find movies that appeal to men; movies such as *Braveheart*, *Gladiator* or *Star Wars*. We talked earlier about how his brain works more in compartments and boxes, rather than interconnected like a woman's brain.

Doctors working at Yale University used magnetic resonance imaging to study the brains of men and women. The men used mostly one section on one side of the brain known as the left inferior gyrus, while women used several areas on both sides of their brains. The book *Brain Sex* by Anne Moir and David Jessel explains how we are differently wired from the womb. In the early weeks of gestation a boy baby is affected in the womb by testosterone, which creates this more structured male brain. He is literally brainwashed.

Men are more 'single-minded' — brain activity focuses in different sections of the brain, and they switch from section to

He will make decisions when he has a plan.

section, like someone moving from appliance to appliance in a house, switching them on when needed and then turning them off.

Women's brains function more 'globally' — they've switched on everything in the house and left it on! This probably accounts for the fact that men can generally focus on tasks very well, and do not notice distractions. His is a world of things: how they work, the space they occupy. His brain leads him to tackle problems in a practical and an inherently self-interested way. This inherent pragmatism leads him often to exercise dominance and power in a relationship.

This strength is very often what is attractive about him, and drew his wife to him in the first place, yet when his wife assumes that he thinks the same way as she does it often becomes a source of frustration to them both. When a man and a woman cannot 'decode' each other, their relationship comes to grief.

> When a man and a woman can decode each other, they can truly learn to compromise and negotiate.

His strengths — your gift

A man's tendency to problem solve and execute a plan is the greatest strength in your relationship. Give a man a plan and he will make it happen. If your husband arrives home at night exhausted and things tend to unwind at that time each day, give him a plan. Ask him to hug you first and then as you connect give him an update on where everything is at, and what the plan is until tea time. Explain to him how the children are waiting for him to come

When a man and a woman cannot 'decode' each other, their relationship comes to grief.

home each night and give him a plan so, for example, when he comes in the door, he plays with them in a focused way for a short period of time. Tell him after that the children can wash up and he can have a few minutes' quiet before tea. He will understand this plan, when you explain if he doesn't give the children that positive attention, they will hunt him down all night anyway!

Men love to solve problems — his ears will glow when you ask for his help to solve a problem. So instead of sharing a tale of woe, ask him for his help. Spell out the problem as you see it and ask him for a solution.

Men tend to be passive and laid-back when it comes to building relationships and their language is often misread by their mates, who see things in more relational terms. Usually if a man is watching a sports game, it will be the game that totally absorbs him whereas his wife might be interested in the players as people.

Why women are so valuable in relationships

A woman is more likely to evaluate relationships accurately and she often has better instincts about people. That doesn't mean that she is always right in that area, as they are only instincts, but her ability to evaluate what is going on gives her an advantage in reading people. I always say to husbands, 'You sleep with a relationship expert every night, so ask her what she thinks.' A woman's brain is especially well suited for interplay with others and her relationships tend to be more complementary than competitive.

hot tip ✔

Courtesy is part of sensitivity and means a lot. Equality between the sexes doesn't negate the giving of courtesy or the delight in receiving it. Open the door, practise the 'after you' on trains or buses, and go the extra mile to ensure that everything is all right. Little things like this matter. They are a mark of respect and care.

Women are more alert to touch, sound and smells. Whereas a man will seek to integrate and understand what he sees, women will focus on and remember more detail. If a couple is driving down a street, a husband might comment on the fact that the whole subdivision is a similar age and has houses built to similar designs, whereas his wife might better remember detail, such as the colour of curtains and landscaping of individual houses.

A woman's brain is designed to excel at networking and cooperation. She can often get the best out of people by helping them to work together. Because they are able to coordinate many different areas of operation and work across a spectrum of relationships, women have always been valuable in small business administration or organisations where cooperation is vital.

Her strengths – your gift

The great strength of a woman is that she has a natural desire to create and nurture good relationships. If you move a metre in a relationship with your wife there is every chance that she will move a kilometre. Because she has a natural tendency to want to make relationships work, she will respond to overtures that she senses are sincere. She can often sense when a relationship is needing attention or when a family dynamic is unravelling or an office relationship is dysfunctional or unhealthy.

Communicating in a way that works for you both

If a wife feels understood, she will respond to that empathy. Our daughter shared recently how, after a long day with a colicky baby and a super-active toddler, she was just about at breaking point. As her husband was about to leave the house that evening for an appointment, she poured out to him how awful her life was. She said his response was unexpected, yet was just what she needed to hear. He stood there and, looking at her with understanding said, 'It must be hard!' She shared how if he had tried to solve her problem or give her advice or even help at that moment, it wouldn't have been as comforting as the acknowledgement of the load she was carrying. If husbands learn the language of understanding, they will be well on the way to opening the channels for love and communication with their wives.

Another friend tells how in frustration she arrived home and burst in the door, pouring out her troubles to her husband. The way he replied surprised her and immediately dissipated her stress and made her want to hug him. He produced a hot drink then said, 'It sounds as if you are upset and frustrated. Tell me about it.'

> There will come to every marriage a time when we are called to love not 'because of' but 'in spite of'. It has at its heart not just the feeling of love but the will to love.
>
> **Rob Parsons,** *The Sixty Minute Marriage*

Refrain from judging your partner for who they are. Their maleness or femaleness or personality traits may be irritating, but is anyone going to die because of them? Accepting your partner is another way of letting go of your fears and experiencing love in the fullest sense. When you learn to accept your partner for what they are and not want to change them, you will also accept yourself.

Remember what is important to a man

A man wants to be affirmed as a man. He doesn't want to feel a wimp or be regarded as such. The hen-pecked husband is not merely a figment of the cartoonist's imagination. A man treated this way will never become the husband that you want.

When he does a poor job of putting on a baby's nappy or making the bed, don't ridicule his attempts or laugh about it at dinner parties. Be proud that he is trying and tell him first of all that you appreciate that, then show him how to put the nappy on like a 'pro'!

Affirming a man, as a man, may require discernment of how he thinks. He may feel that his manhood is fulfilled in sporting prowess, in success at work, in a DIY hobby or in taking responsibility on outings. When you as his wife take pleasure in encouraging him wherever possible, you will support him as a man.

We spoke to a young husband recently who had broken up with his wife. He made some interesting observations from his pain and personal journey. I was particularly struck by one comment. He said, 'You know, we men are actually quite easily managed. We just need the pat on the back and some kind words every now and again.' He explained how the put-down is so painful. It stings and burns at the core.

Some things to remember:

- *When your husband becomes uncaring or distant towards you it is usually because he is afraid of something.*
- *A lot of the time, he will 'report', more than converse. Just think about his telephone manner. Usually his comments are brief, utilitarian and to the point. 'Okay. Got it . . . Be there at eight . . . See you soon.'*
- *Understand that a man is more motivated to achieve goals than to absorb moments. He also wants to manage his own problems and be 'Mr Fix-it'.*
- *Try not to be offended by his impatience to get to the bottom line in a discussion — it's a natural male instinct.*
- *And always remember — a man fears nothing more than failure.*

Remember what is important to a woman

Appreciate that your partner needs to feel you value her beyond all your other human relationships, because she values relational moments far more than occupational achievements.

And always remember that a woman is deeply affirmed when a man makes a noticeable effort to hear her heart.

Understand that your partner needs to feel free to share her opinion and to help you understand where she is coming from without you getting frustrated or angry. She needs to feel she can trust you.

Personality differences

Extroverts and introverts have very different emotional needs. They relax in different ways and they often don't understand each other very well. Extroverts tend to think as they are talking, and to put everything out on the table (as the wife of an author friend of ours who is a great extrovert once said, 'Every thought my husband has ever had has been published!'). Extroverts tend to be 'open books' and often have lots of friends and acquaintances. They are energised by people and activity. Introverts, on the other hand, often need time to put their thoughts into words. They are more likely to have a few deep friendships than many acquaintances and they need space and sensitivity to recharge and regain equilibrium as too much 'people contact' can drain them of emotional energy.

There are a variety of courses and books on the subject of personality styles and we do not have time to go into it in depth here as it is really a whole subject in itself.[7] However, understanding and valuing what the other brings into your marriage within their personality style is foundational to enjoying each other. Human beings are motivated by very different triggers and environments and acknowledging the underlying emotional needs of each other will help you work things out as you both enjoy the marriage experience.

Young friends of our acquaintance would drive each other spare

hot tip ✔

- Try encouraging your husband to participate by offering him a plan and a choice: 'How about you take the children to sport and I'll do the shopping, or we can swap.'
- If you don't feel like saying loving words, say something that is true and kind as well. It might be just how thankful you are that your spouse takes responsibility for delivering the children to school each morning.

with the way they barbecued when they entertained friends. As the husband was carefully turning the sausages half a turn every few minutes so that he kept an eye on their progress, his wife would be welcoming people at the door — telling a funny story and throwing another sausage on the barbecue, messing up his methodical system and frustrating his plan. She loved people and enjoyed the fun and activity of their company and the cooking or any plan that it involved was incidental to her. He took it personally as a huge insensitivity on her part and she just couldn't 'get' what he was on about.

He couldn't believe how she would come home from the supermarket and start baking before she had finished unpacking then suddenly think of a phone call she needed to make to tell a friend a piece of news. To him that was incomprehensible because he always finished one thing before he moved on to another. He had loved her spontaneity when they first met, but this way of flitting from task to task was beginning to drive him crazy. At the same time she wondered why he would take the dog for a walk when he was stressed. She felt abandoned as affection was very important to her and when she was upset, she just wanted hugs and closeness, not distance.

Learning about personality differences and the way they were wired made the difference to this couple. They learnt to laugh at each other's need for certain things and make allowances for their personality bents. For example the husband was a 'beaver' type of personality. He needed order and predictability and a sense of how it was done before, in the way he operated. He also sometimes needed space and sensitivity in order to recharge and regroup in his mind. His basic motivation was 'Let's do it the right way'. His wife was a classic 'otter' type personality whose greatest needs were attention,

hot tip ✔

Purchase a book on personality types and read it together. Act on your new knowledge.

affection and approval. Her basic motivation was 'Let's do it the fun way'. To miss each other in this way can be tragic. For this couple this one insight that highlighted their underlying needs was life-defining and they say to this day that it saved their marriage.

You may have loved your partner's gregariousness when you first met them, but be going crazy because they are constantly inviting their whole family around to watch a rugby match or organising whole groups of friends into camping holidays. These differences are not wrong — they are an opportunity for you to get some insight into each other and negotiate a way in which you can both live with those differences.

Different personality types have different emotional needs. People feel loved when there is some understanding of these differing needs.

What motivates you? What motivates your partner?

The story is told of paratroopers jumping out of a plane. As one jumped out, his parachute opened and he floated confidently towards the ground. He was just starting to enjoy the view when the other, desperately pulling his unresponsive rip cord, screamed past him in free fall. The first one looked at him speeding past, and said, 'So it's a race you want' — as he struggled out of his

hot tip ✔

Do you and your partner fully understand your own and each other's motives? Get together and draw up a list of the things that are your top motivations; those things that you love and do to reward yourself.

parachute harness!

It is amazing what will motivate us. For some, a challenge of any sort must be responded to!

When we understand each other's motivations we are so much better equipped to negotiate a compromise than when we are just fighting for what we want or for what makes us feel comfortable.

Sally and John had been married approximately 18 months when they went looking for help over an ongoing power struggle. They were a high-achieving young couple, both working hard in corporate jobs during the week. As a rule they relaxed socially in some way with friends on Friday nights, but by Saturday morning, each week without fail, they came to grief over the same issue.

Sally wanted them both to stay home, do the chores, pay the bills and get their lives in order. John, however, had different ideas. He wanted to go out and play sport, do something with his friends, have fun.

They both considered that what they were wanting was a reasonable way to reward themselves after a hard week's work. Sally had grown up in a family that had moved house often, and she had a deep need for security. Her introverted personality also meant that the way she wound down was through having space, order and creativity in her life. John, on the other hand, was a highly sociable young man. He loved fun, was a surfer, a sports fanatic and always the life of the party. His way of winding down and rewarding himself after a big week was to go out and have fun; to play sport and see his mates. It is not too hard to see why Saturday morning was a power struggle over what they should do.

This distressed couple discovered a very simple but powerful exercise. They took a few minutes to write down their motivations, from the strongest at the top to the least important at the bottom. You will see from the chart below that their motivations were almost directly opposite to each other.

John	**Sally**
Leisure	Security
Fun	Bills paid
Sport	Chores, order
Friends	Creativity
Family	Peace, space
Work	Family and friends
Order	Work
Security	Leisure

Love relationships are like two people dancing. Understanding motivations is another step in the dance routine. It gives us the chance to show understanding and appreciation of the other person, who has abilities that we don't possess. This couple could make decisions to exclude each other from certain parts of their lives, fighting for their own needs, or they could sit down and talk.

They could look at the list of motivations and say to each other 'How can we work this out in such a way that we can both live with it?'

Sally works hard in order to create space to make sure her life is in order. John works hard in order to go out and have fun.

When they realised what their motivations were — and accepted that their differences needed to be part of the equation — then both could operate safely.

Their decision was to incorporate both sets of needs into their day. They decided to spend the first part of the morning together. John does the Saturday breakfast in bed and together they do the essential chores. Later in the day John goes out to play sport and see his mates, while Sally enjoys her 'space' and creative time. John is happy for her to look after the household finances, because she is good at them and because this gives her the security she needs.

People who have successful marriages have built partnerships that allow for each other's differences and autonomy.

Love languages – ways of expressing and receiving love

> Love looks not with the eyes, but with the mind.
>
> **William Shakespeare,** *A Midsummer Night's Dream*

Many people are trying harder to communicate their love to their spouse, when perhaps they should be trying differently. When our son was newly married, his young wife would get upset on occasions, after she had been to a lot of trouble to cook a beautiful meal. He would come home and instead of sitting down to eat it immediately, would give her a long affectionate hug. He wanted to show her how appreciative he was by hugging her; having come from a hugging family, it seemed natural to him. However, her language of love was *acts of service* and she got upset at his delay

Action lab

Offer your spouse a 'Honey Do' day

- *Schedule a Saturday (or a day off work) to work around the house.*
- *Enlist the children's help or find a place for them to spend the day.*
- *Build anticipation. Five days before the workday, give your spouse a scroll tied with a ribbon and ask them to write down three things that they would like done around the house. Read it out aloud and after reading each one, bow to them with a smile, saying something like, 'As you wish'.*

Plan to take your spouse on their favourite excursion

- *Schedule a weekend away and arrange for the children to be cared for.*
- *A week or two before the date, give him or her a passport using one of their old photographs and a supposed airline ticket to an island off the coast of your city.*
- *Book a fishing trip for you both or another adventure they would enjoy, like a four-wheel-driving expedition.*
- *Take a picnic lunch to enjoy afterwards.*

in sitting down to enjoy the meal. She felt genuinely loved and appreciated when he valued her *act* of making the meal. Such a simple cross-communication and misunderstanding caused them real perception problems for a while, until they learned what was going on. His language of love (*physical touch and closeness*) was so different to her language of love. In fact it was as if one of them was speaking Swahili and the other Chinese!

hot tip ✓

- Talk about your languages of love on a date night or over a meal.
- Try to identify each other's language of love and ask what thing you currently do for them that makes them feel most loved.

Different but not wrong

It is not uncommon for a couple to visit a marriage counsellor and as she pours out her heart about how her husband doesn't listen to her, or take time to take her out, he becomes angry and frustrated. He bursts out, 'There's not a tap in the house that leaks, I mow the lawns every week, I've just painted the house. What else does she want?'

He is trying hard to please her in the way that he wants to be loved, through *acts of service*, but she is longing for *quality time and attention* and so they are missing each other and consequently feeling unloved by the other.

There are many ways of showing love and affection, but we tend to have a preferred love language — the one we use most often. It is also usually the love language that we prefer others to use with us. However, it may not be the way that our spouse feels loved. In our early days together I would buy Mary gifts when I had been away but, although she acknowledged the thought behind them, because of our tight budget they made her feel guilty. She would have felt more loved if I had given her more quality time and attention. I have since learned the value of knowing her love language and operating in ways that she really appreciates. Understanding the love languages can help bring relationships alive. A young husband recently joked that after expressing his

Remember someone must take the initiative – do not wait for love before you love.

love to his new wife by bringing small gifts home regularly, he suspected 'acts of service' may elicit a warmer response. He said that he had quickly discovered that 'ironing his own shirts' was a winning act of foreplay in his wife's mind!

There are five languages of love which we tend to operate in and hopefully we operate in them all at different times. But one of them is your primary language of love and speaks to you more deeply on the emotional level than the others. If you are a person who needs words of encouragement and your spouse faithfully does things for you but never actually says anything warmly appreciative of you, your love bank may suffer. Operating in his or her 'native' language of love, as it were, will top up that love bank.

The languages of love

- *Gift-giving*
- *Acts of service*
- *Words of encouragement*
- *Quality time and attention*
- *Physical touch and closeness*

As we recognise the love that others are trying to show us, and learn how to love them in ways that they will appreciate the most, misunderstandings in the communication of love will reduce. One of our children is a real gift-giver, another will feel really loved if you take her out for a coffee and a talk (love language — quality time and attention), and the other really needs words of encouragement. It is important, when your partner needs love the

hot tip ✔

- Continue to keep your relationship a 'we' business.
- Process the data as quickly as possible and talk *with* your partner — not *at* them.
- Celebrate your victories. 'We were totally at odds there and yes, it was tense for a while. But we overcame the hurdle.'
- Check that you have not become negative about each other and allowed that negativity to influence your view of each other.

most, to love them in their language rather than yours.

The couple we spoke of in the first chapter, Kate and Peter, had got stuck because Kate's love language was very gift-orientated. She felt unloved and unvalued because her husband and his family had not worked out that a thoughtful gift was really significant to her.

> Love is not just an emotion, it is an action.

My attitude can influence everything

If we allow our negative emotions to control our behaviour, we will feel even more negative. A positive attitude, however, and kind actions, can influence our spouse's emotions positively and change everything. Remember someone must take the initiative — do not wait for love before you love. Being grateful every day for the good things in your life and expressing that gratefulness will lift your happiness quotient and that of your family's.

CHAPTER 11

More about romance and enjoyment

In the all-important world of family relations, three words are almost as powerful as the famous 'I love you'. They are 'Maybe you're right'.

Oren Arnold

Romance is sending out a message to your mate about how special and desirable he is. It is recognising his sexuality in and out of the bedroom. It's the recognition of your femininity and his masculinity. It is stopping in the mad rush of life to focus on your partner as unique.

Wilfred Arlan Peterson, *The Art of Marriage*

If you are capable of growing into the largeness of marriage, do it.

Jesus Christ, *The Message Bible*

Keeping the passion alive

Emotions cannot be commanded to appear but they will come freely when the conditions are right. Every person on this earth needs romance. Romance means that you matter to me more than anything else; more than my friends, colleagues, my work or my hobbies, and I will seek you out to lavish my love on. Build romantic love on your side of the marriage by thinking about your partner, concentrating on positive experiences and pleasures out of the past and then day-dreaming, anticipating future pleasure with your mate. At the same time, work on providing the right emotional climate for your spouse's romantic love to grow.

And it is interesting how attractive that ideal of human love is. When we see a man who has sustained his passion and love for his wife over many years, we are enchanted. The 'happily ever after' of storybooks means in reality that a man and woman's love for each other remains romantic, passionate and exclusive even over many years of familiarity, the birth of children and the sagging of various body parts.

There are some lovely moments in Ranulph Fiennes's 2007 autobiography, *Mad, Bad and Dangerous to Know,* when both he and his first wife talk about their love for each other. His wife Ginny says, 'I think of Ran as my very closest, dearest friend as well as my husband. It's hell when he's away and he's a wonderful person to be with.' And when she was in the last stages of cancer, he recalls,

'I will never forget that time. I cannot believe that any human has ever loved another as much as I loved and still love Ginny. I could not remember any time in my adult life when she was not the reason for the glow in my heart when we were together, and the longed for safe haven during my wanderings without her.'

Immortal Wife by Irving Stone is the story of Jessie Benton Fremont and her marriage to John Charles Fremont, who won fame as a fearless explorer and a figure who left his mark on every major event in nineteenth-century America.

At 16 Jessie fell in love with Fremont. She never got over that love. She used it to make a marriage that was for them an indestructible third entity helping them build victory from every defeat.

'Thirty years of marriage had deepened rather than exhausted their sense of pleasure in each other; the delight at a new hair style, the way a dress or suit fitted, the adroit expression of an idea, the slow, warm, approving smile on a face whose every expression was better known than one's own image in the mirror.

'In three decades of marriage they had gone through so much together, both of success and failure, that they were carved into each other's memory; there was gratitude here, but gratitude would not have been enough to engender the closeness and delight of their spirits. During the harassed and unhappy war years they had relearned that trouble and passion are poor bedfellows; now, in the easy, joyful comfort of creative years, when their last ambitions were pushing forward toward completion, their physical love flared anew.'

Have a lifelong affair with your mate

With kids, a house and a career, where do you take time to be a couple? Rediscover how to court one another, and have fun together. Make space for each other. Get away! Retreat! Hide! It's good for you and your family. There are few pleasures as reliable as a few days away from the family you love.

Take a quiet walk, escape for dinner and a movie; get away for the weekend. Don't underestimate the payoff for you as a couple for the energy it may take to orchestrate romantic time together. A dad of four who told us of the resistance he met from his wife when he suggested he book a hotel room for a night on their wedding anniversary, says when he gave her time to think about it and organise some practical details, she warmed to the idea and they experienced one of their loveliest memories. The quiet morning of breakfast reading and chatting together, without the overlay of family activity, was an enjoyable treat in their busy lives. Another husband told how he booked his wife and mother of five into a hotel room all on her own for a day and night. He ordered coffee for her, and a book by her favourite author, and left her to enjoy 24 hours of uninterrupted peace. He was well rewarded when he arrived in the morning to the enthusiastic welcome from his grateful and responsive wife!

Take regular 'newmoons'–a married version of a honeymoon.

Making time for play

Don't allow your marriage to get into a rut. It is not very sensitive to fall into the same old unchanging routines, the same old clothes and boring ways of doing things. Introduce special occasions, celebrations and unexpected treats, like weekends away. It does both partners good to dress up and go out together. There is so much to enjoy in this wonderful world. Remember the eye contact, the touching, the unexpected hug. Kiss in a crowded area. An airport is a fun way to stage a reunion. If you are there to meet someone, arrive early and run towards each other as if this is a reunion after weeks not just minutes or hours!

Dance in your living room by candlelight. Write a love note in lipstick on the mirror. Put perfume on the sheets. Be generous with compliments. Send a love letter through the mail. Write a poem.

And make a habit of thanking your partner for thoughtful actions, for cooking nice meals, for reading to the children or even for reliably performing mundane chores like putting out the rubbish and putting petrol in the car. Serve one another — it is a guaranteed way to reduce tensions and to help build passion.

Research suggests that few people 'jump the fence' from a marriage, just for sex. The catalyst is actually a need for recreational activities and excitement, with sex as the outcome. Such a need is often caused by partners taking each other for granted, leading to indifference, which can lead to a search for new experiences.

Tell your wife you think that she is beautiful and tell your husband how handsome and attractive you find him. Laugh together. A great sense of humour is sexy and keeps your mate on board. Tell him you love his body and were thinking about him all day. Tell him you are so proud of what he does and how he cares for the family.

Notice and tell her you appreciate the way she does so many little things that others may not notice.

If couples are sexually in love with one another they are more willing to see the other side of the other person. They'll be more gentle, more caring, less judgemental and demanding.

The grass *can* look decidedly greener on your side of the fence. Tell your wife you think she is beautiful and sexy. Tell your husband you think he's handsome and attractive.

Exhaustion and modern lifestyles

Exhaustion can be a romance killer. If both partners have only the dregs at the end of the day then escalation of conflict, exclusion of the other and the fading of romance are the result. In cities the stress of spending hours in the car, whether it is travelling to work or taxiing children about, takes a toll on both partners' emotional energy. Many psychologists are concluding that life, as we expect it today, is not conducive to marriage. Two careers and children all at the same time is a very hard equation to juggle.

You may need to look at your life and do a trade-off for a few years in the number of hours you work outside the home, in order to keep your energy levels sufficient to nurture your family in the realities of modern life. For a 'season' one of you may need to think about reducing your working hours until it feels comfortable and both commit to taking a family day once a week to keep a balance in your life.

Take regular weekend or overnight getaways, with no friends, relatives or children. It can be anywhere except in your own home. You may feel that you can't afford regular weekends away; that your budget is just too tight, and what about neglecting the children? Have you thought how much it will cost you if you don't take time out for each other?

There are two truths that may help you to look at the importance of romance in a new light. One is that the happiest, most well-adjusted children come from homes where mum and dad

> If couples are sexually in love they tend to be more caring . . . and less judgemental and demanding of each other.

love each other and have time for each other. The other is that if you do neglect your relationship, the cost in anxiety, stress, loneliness, counsellors' fees or a divorce will be far higher than the cost of a weekend at a special hotel or getaway.

It is a popular saying that you only go around once, and life is for living. See your life as a series of 'seasons'. If you have to drive an older-model car for a few years (you may have to do that anyway if your marriage collapses), in order to enjoy a quality friendship with your spouse and time with your kids, then so be it.

hot tip ✓

Give each other a gift every day in the form of a thoughtful favour. It might be just to do the dishes!

Idealisation of the other tends to be a component in happy marriages

Early idealisations remain very powerful. A strong, romantic, in-love feeling early in a marriage tends to be the glue in many happy marriages.

Although he has since experienced a tumultuous and very public disastrous second marriage, Sir Paul McCartney expressed this type of love when speaking about his first wife Linda, who died in 1998 from breast cancer.

Often wearing baggy clothes and little make-up, she wasn't a standout beauty, but McCartney, close to tears in an interview after Linda's death, said, 'We fancied each other something rotten. To me, she was always still my girlfriend.'

Though marriage brings plenty of opportunities to scrutinise each other's faults, it seems better to view each other through rose-tinted spectacles than microscopes.

One couple who spent several months early in their marriage exploring Italian paddocks, Romanian forests and the art galleries of the Continent say that they had every possible argument in those early days in the confined environment of their campervan. But they had huge adventures: 'Those early experiences bind us together. Our children benefit because they see that if I am not with Jim I really miss him. I see that as a real sign of our love.'

You chose your love, now choose to love your choice

Feelings will change over the course of a lifetime and there will be times when you may not feel that your needs are being met or even that you love this person any more. That is the time to commit to whatever it takes to reconnect, just as you would with any other enterprise in which you are engaged. We may not feel like feeding our children each day or getting up and going to work, but when we do what is necessary, then we are often invigorated by doing it. Maybe you don't feel like a few days on the beach or like organising a trip away — but if your marriage requires it, then you must do it. And the feeling of invigoration and reconnection as lovers and friends after a week in the sun, or cosied up together by

hot tip ✓

- Leave a loving voicemail message on your partner's cellphone, which they can listen to throughout the day.
- Create a collection of date coupons that your spouse can redeem throughout the year. Think of things that would surprise or please them, like a back rub, a favourite home-cooked meal (plus dessert!), an afternoon of uninterrupted time to watch sports, or maybe instant forgiveness for one of their little irksome habits.
- Pick up your favourite dinner-to-go and try a change of venue. Dine outside in the backyard.
- Make a date to go to the gym together.

a log fire, will be your reward.

Feelings will often take us down a self-destructive track. We may not feel like putting in a full day's work, but our business requires it. In the same way, our marriage requires that we give it priority. If we neglect our spouse then we are saying that other things matter more.

Even the most passionate relationship tends to mellow out over the years and what was once an exciting adventure can become a comfortable routine. While there is nothing wrong with that, in relationships where passion is more of a memory than a reality, you can still regain that 'life of its own' for your relationship. Think about whatever you did to attract your spouse. Do it just as wholeheartedly to keep them!

Spontaneity

Every once in a while break loose — do something impulsive. Like setting off in the car for a day with nothing planned. Stop where and when you want, explore new territory, enjoy totally new experiences.

If you have to go away on business, leave intimate notes and messages taped around the house, where they will be discovered by your partner.

If your budget prevents you from hiring a babysitter and enjoying a night out, cook a special dinner for your partner and serve it in the dining room you have magically transformed into a 'mood' restaurant. Follow this with a concert of selected music in the lounge, then a dance on the patio and a bubble bath.

Honour each other

Treat your husband or wife as an honoured guest. Welcome them as someone special and their arrival as the highlight of your day.

Remember that a phone call can be rescheduled or concluded. If a television personality came to the door, would you ignore him or her? What about the neighbour or a tradesperson; would you continue to talk on the phone or would you drop everything to greet them? Watch the feelings change as you show honour to the one you love.

Action lab

- *Write down three things that you appreciate about your spouse.*
- *Write down one thing you would love him or her to do for you.*

Dreaming and using your imagination

Playing the 'What?' game is a great way for partners to regain some dreams and reconnect at heart level.

- What is your best memory of your mother? Your father?
- What was your favourite year in school?
- What are your three favourite movies of all time?
- What's the one thing you'd like to be remembered for?
- What is your dream job?
- If you had more time, what hobby would you like to pursue?
- If you only had one week to live what would you do?

Marriages change

> People change but they forget to tell each other.
>
> **Lillian Hellman,** playwright

As we mature and grow, our marriages will change. It is interesting to note that women especially grow by changing. Very often men are confused by this because they expect everything to stay the same. They thought they had a deal when they married but now it seems to him as if she has shifted the goalposts — and overnight to boot, while he was sleeping!

What is important is that you renegotiate with your spouse if you have plans for a change. You may decide that you would like to return to work, pursue more education, have another child, etc. Then renegotiate with your spouse. Take him out for a date and talk to him. Ask him what he thinks about the idea.

Remember his predisposition for problem solving and fixing things. So present the issue as a problem; that you are feeling

hot tip ✔

Catch your spouse by surprise by interrupting the normal routine and expressing the wonderful truth you feel deep inside.

restless, for example, and ready for a new challenge, and ask him to help with solutions. Use **the floor** if necessary. Give him time to get used to a new idea. If he is adamantly opposed, then give him space to think about it and return to the idea in a week or so. If he is totally unhappy and you think his reasons are not valid, then think of how you can achieve the same goal in a different way.

We should all have three marriages in our lifetime . . . but with the same person!

Affairs – a reality check

Our permissive world makes it very easy to stray from remaining faithful and investing solely in our marriages. Today's media portrayals of no-strings casual sexual relationships are challenges that every marriage will face. The permissive society appears to approve or at least accept them. But tragically the outcomes are still the same as they have been for thousands of years: betrayal, guilt, shattered lives for children and years of complications.

Is it worth the excitement and sexual intrigue that an affair appears to offer? Counsellors who deal in this area tend to wholeheartedly demur. They ask if the short-term pleasure is worth the long-term pain. They suggest that the sex may be incredible, and the conversation captivating in this exciting new relationship,

> Imagine yourself telling your spouse, parents and children that you have been unfaithful.

but at some point the principle will come into effect that will rock them to their heels. 'The grass on the other side of the fence may look greener — but one day it too will have to be mowed!' As Rob Parsons says in his book *The Sixty Minute Marriage*, 'The ordinary will invade their lives. Who would have thought that the tap would have leaked here in this new life as it always did in the bathroom at home? Who could have predicted an evening when one of them would say, "No, not tonight. And did you put the rubbish out?" Who could have told him that he would begin to dream of telling his children a story or bandaging a cut knee? He knows little of that now as he stands in the hallway with his brand new cases on his way to his brand new relationship, in his search for the person who will fulfil his dreams.'

If you are tempted to stray, even the most alluring situation can be brought into perspective if you imagine yourself telling your spouse, parents and children what you have done. Every effective trap is disguised by an attractive bait. The bait may look wonderful but the hook of long-term consequences will be real.

It's hard to think of that when the illusion first hits. But perhaps George Bernard Shaw was right: 'There are two tragedies in life: one is to lose your heart's desire. The other is to gain it.'

The big rocks in life

A professor, lecturing his students, pulls out from under the bench a large glass jar. Then he produces a paper bag containing fist-sized rocks. Holding one of the rocks in his hand he says to his students,

hot tip ✓

- Decide to do three kind things for your spouse each day. Be surprised to discover that the feelings you may feel have gone, will return. Feelings are just feelings. But your attitude can change them.
- If you don't feel in love – then just *act* in love. If you don't feel like being romantic, do the actions that will create the opportunity for romance.

'How many of these rocks can I place in this jar?' They call out numbers between 10 and 15. Carefully the professor begins to put the rocks in the jar until they reach the top. He says to the students, 'Is the jar full?' and they respond 'Yes'.

He then searches again under the bench and pulls out a bag of pebbles. He begins pouring the pebbles into the jar and they filter around the rocks until they reach the top. He asks the students again, 'Is the jar full?' Catching on, they respond, 'No'. At which point he brings out a bag of sand and pours it into the jar until that too reaches the top. 'Is it full now?' They, of course, call out 'No'.

Then he reaches for a jug of water and pours it over everything already in the jar until it meets the top. He repeats his question 'Is it full?' And finally they acknowledge, 'Yes'.

He then asks the students what great life lesson they have learnt from that experiment. The answers ranged from, 'Everything counts no matter how big' to 'It takes all sorts of experiences to make up life'.

The professor smiles and says, 'I want you never to forget this lesson. It may be the most significant thing you ever learn about life. If you don't get the big rocks in first, you will never get them in.' The key is to work out what your life's big rocks are: marriage, career, friendship, family, to name a few.

In marriage we all know how easy it is to allow the small everyday things of life — the sand and the pebbles, to crowd out the 'big' rocks.

We encourage you to re-evaluate often whether you are still prioritising and valuing the 'big rocks'.

hot tip ✓

One friend has told us that the idea that has impacted the most on their marriage is that of 'cloth napkin' dinners. From the earliest days of their marriage they have committed to two dinners a week where they sit down to dine and talk together, with the table fully laid with candles and cloth napkins. They say no other single decision has been so important in their lives together. They now give their friends who are getting married cloth napkins with the story of what a 'cloth napkin' dinner is pinned to the card.

Doing it alone can be too hard

We have already mentioned the wider family and community as a garden that can support your marriage. We also believe that a spiritual community or family, such as a positive church, offers friendship, programmes and mentors for you and your children, as well as ongoing teaching and inspiration about living life well.

It is this knowledge that there is a loving personal God who designed men and women to live together and nurture each other that has helped Mary and me so much over the years. Knowing there is a God who offers His love and help in good times and in bad has been one of the strengths of our marriage. As I often joke in seminars, my most common prayer as a husband has been, 'Dear God, it's me again. I am in the "Winnie the Pooh" — not much Winnie!' I have found that God can handle prayers like that.

Years ago when I was a young radio technician working the doggo shift (midnight to 8am) at Makara radio station in Wellington, we received an urgent call from the air ministry. It was during the era when they were setting up the Deep Freeze operation in Antarctica. An eight-engine Skymaster plane had got into trouble. It had enough fuel to fly to McMurdo Sound but not enough for a safe return flight. The plane had flown to Antarctica, but just before landing, a blizzard hit and it was unable to land, forcing it to return to Christchurch. The crisis was whether they would make it back. Someone had come up with the idea that because of the time difference, the designers of this plane would possibly be contactable in the US and could give expert advice to the captain.

In those days, all overseas telephone conversations were transmitted on shortwave radio and were scrambled so that no one could listen in; a decision was made to remove the scrambler, allowing us to listen to the conversation and keep the circuit as clear as possible.

Even after all these years I feel emotions welling up as I recount the experience. To hear the two designers, from Lockheed, talking passionately about their big baby and giving advice on the tolerances of such things as fuel gauges was gripping. As the drama proceeded they offered advice to the crew on the most efficient altitude at which to fly and ways to conserve fuel to increase the possibility of getting the aircraft back to an airstrip capable of handling it.

I can still hear the coolness of the captain's voice, but also the controlled passion of the designers to get their plane back no matter what. I can still see us two radio technicians cheering when that great Skymaster plane landed at Christchurch airport, in the early hours of the morning, with probably only ounces of kerosene sloshing in its tank!

I often think of that experience and how turning to the designer averted a disaster. We would suggest that, in marriage, the designer who thought up love, sex and intimacy, in the beginning, would know something about it.

As in John Milton's classic *Paradise Lost*, where Adam asks God for a life's companion who is different from him because otherwise it would be self-worship and also for someone who is equal, because only an equal can be a true friend, there is no other relationship so satisfying to our human need of completeness through relationship with another than marriage.

Marriage is the ultimate growing experience

The golden standard of love in marriage can be summed up in what is often read at marriage ceremonies — the love chapter from the Bible. Here it is in a modern version:

> Love never gives up
> Love cares more for others than for self
> Love doesn't want what it doesn't have
> Love doesn't strut, doesn't have a swelled head, doesn't fly off the handle

Doesn't keep score of others, doesn't revel when others grovel
Takes pleasure in the flowering of truth
Puts up with anything
Trusts God always, always looks for the best
Never looks back, but keeps on going to the end.

1 Corinthians 13

The Message, translation of the *Bible*

As we conclude, we were thinking about the very best of what marriage can bring and it reminded us of a reading at one of our children's weddings (we haven't yet been able to track down the source) which articulated it so well.

'The love of a man for a woman and a woman for a man has been celebrated throughout the ages and across the world's various cultures. Loveliness and beauty, devotion and sacrifice are evoked in the lyrical and passionate expression of our humanity. What ideal of human love is more beautiful than a man and woman committed to each other and delighting in each other. One of the loveliest examples of that love is the couple whose faithful partnership is unbroken over many years — through all the ups and downs, the joys and the sorrows that life brings.'

Bibliography

Arndt, B, *The Sex Diaries: Why Women Go Off Sex and Other Bedroom Battles*, Melbourne University Press, Melbourne, 2009.

Brizendine, L, *The Female Brain*, Morgan Road Books, USA, 2006.

Chapman, G, *Loving Solutions*, Northfield Publishing, USA, 1998.

Clatworthy, N, article in *Seventeen*. The Case Against Living Together November 1977.

Edwards, K, *The Memory Keeper's Daughter*, Penguin, New York, 2005.

Eldridge, J, *Wild at Heart: Discovering the Secret of a Man's Soul*, Thomas Nelson, Inc., Nashville, Tennessee, 2001.

Farrel, B & P Farrel, *Men are Like Waffles — Women are Like Spaghetti*, Harvest House Publishers, Eugene, Oregon, 2001.

Fiennes, R, *Mad, Bad and Dangerous to Know*, Hodder & Stoughton, London, 2007.

Fisher, H, *Anatomy of Love*, WW Norton & Co, New York, 1992.

Gottman, JM & RW Levenson, 'A two-factor model for predicting when a couple will divorce: exploratory analyses using 14-year longitudinal data', *Family Process*, vol. 41, no. 1, 2002, pp. 83–96.

Harley, Dr W, *Fall in Love, Stay in Love*, Fleming H. Revell, Ada, Michigan, 2001.

Lewis, CS, *The Four Loves*, Collins, Fontana, London, 1960.

Lindbergh, AM, *Hour of Gold, Hour of Lead: Diaries and Letters of Anne Morrow Lindbergh, 1929–1932*, Mariner Books, Wilmington, 1993.

Littauer, F, *Personality Plus*, Fleming H. Revell, Grand Rapids, Michigan, 1992 (first published 1983).

Markman, HJ, SL Blumberg & SM Stanley, *Fighting for Your Marriage: Positive Steps for Preventing Divorce and Preserving a Lasting Love*, new and revised ed, John Wiley & Sons, San Francisco, 2001.

Mason, M, *The Mystery of Marriage*, Multnomah Publishers, Oregon, USA, 1985.

Merrill, T & B Sandoz-Merrill, *Settle for More*, SelectBooks, New York, 2005.

Moir, A & D Jessel, *Brain Sex*, Delta, New York, 1989.

Moore, B, *The Luck of Ginger Coffey*, New Canadian Library, Canada, 1988 (first published 1960).

Morley, P, *The Man in the Mirror*, Zondervan Grand Rapid, Michigan, 1989.

Newenhuyse, EC, 'Are We Still in Love?', *The Christian Reader*, vol. 16.

Notarius, C & HJ Markman (eds), *We Can Work it Out: How to Solve Conflicts, Save Your Marriage, and Strengthen Your Love for Each Other*, Penguin, New York, 1994.

O'Connor, J, *Have Your Wedding Cake and Eat it Too*, Thomas Nelson, Nashville, Tennessee, 2002.

Parsons, R, *The Sixty Minute Marriage*, B&H Publishing Group, Nashville, Tennessee, 2001.

Peck, MS, *The Road Less Travelled*, Touchstone, New York, 1978.

Peterson, E, *A Long Obedience in the Same Direction*, InterVarsity Press, Illinois, 1980.

Peterson, WA, *The Art of Marriage*, Souvenir Press Ltd, USA, 2005.

Pollock, J, *Amazing Grace: John Newton's Story*, Harper & Row, New York, 1981.

Stead, WT, *Catherine Booth of the Salvation Army*, James Nisbett & Company, 1979.

Stone, I, *Immortal Wife*, Consolidated Book Publishers, London, 1950.

Waite, LJ, D Browning, WJ Doherty, M Gallagher, Y Luo & SM Stanley, 'Does Divorce Make People Happy? Findings from a study of unhappy marriages', Institute for American Values, New York, 2002.

Wallerstein, J & S Blakeslee, *The Good Marriage*, Warner Books, New York, 1995.

Endnotes

1 The doctor who is notorious for helping patients to suicide or practise euthanasia.

2 Judith Wallerstein & Sandra Blakeslee, *The Good Marriage*, p. 27.

3 *Hour of Gold, Hour of Lead: Diaries and Letters of Anne Morrow Lindbergh, 1929–1932.*

4 Linda J. Waite et al., *Does Divorce Make People Happy? Findings from a study of unhappy marriages*, Institute for American Values, New York, p. 5.

5 An April 2009 Australian ABS trends survey found that women do almost twice as much housework as men — 33 hours 45 mins a week. But while men might not do as much vacuuming and ironing, they spend a lot more time than women working outside the house in paid jobs — an average of 31 hrs 50 mins a week, compared with women's 16 hours 25 mins.

6 WT Stead, *Catherine Booth of the Salvation Army.*

7 A good place to start would be *Personality Plus*, by Florence Littauer